WHAT PEOPl

A SAILC

Serving in the Navy with Paul Quito was a great honor because he is a man of respect and honor. Paul Quito is a true man of God. We worshiped God with music every time we were together during deployment. Also, Paul was a great influence on me and other sailors in our command. He wasn't like the other sailors who partied and drank. He is a Christian who's faithful to God and our Lord and Savior Jesus Christ.

—Kaleb Buller
United States Navy Veteran
Sonar Technician Surface (STG) 3rd Class
Musician

I've gotten to know Andrew over the last ten years or so as his mentor. I met Andrew through his brother Dexter, the worship pastor at the church I pastor. I love daily devotionals—they are valuable spiritual tools to start your day. Andrew has a quiet connection with Holy Spirit that flows onto the pages of this devotional. You will find answers and truth based on questions you have had about yourself and the circumstances you are in. You will relate to Andrew's transparency; it will be like a breath of fresh air and peace each day as you learn more about who God is in our lives.

—Barry Kidd
Pastoral Care at Lighthouse Church in Mount Juliet, TN

A SAILOR'S *JOURNAL*

Published by Dream Releaser Publishing

Cover design by Sara Young
Cover photo by Donna Lynne Atwood

ISBN: 978-1-962401-69-2   1 2 3 4 5 6 7 8 9 10

Printed in the United States of America

70 days of devotion to God's empowering grace

A SAILOR'S JOURNAL

ANDREW QUITO

Dedication

Most importantly, I am grateful for my Lord and Savior, Jesus Christ, to whom all gifts, talent, glory, honor, and praises belong. I dedicate this book to Him.

CONTENTS

FOREWORD

It is with immense pride and joy that I write the foreword for my youngest brother's devotional. Watching him grow from a curious child into a talented author has been one of the greatest pleasures of my life. We didn't have a father growing up. Our mother passed away when he was fourteen years old, and I had the responsibility of parenting him and our middle brother, Leo. His journey is a testament to God's empowering grace.

From the earliest days, my brother possessed a unique ability to see the world through a lens of wonder and possibility. His gentleness and empathy have always set him apart, and these qualities shine through in his writing.

This book is not just a collection of words on pages; it is a labor of love, a culmination of years of experience, and a reflection of growing up in the Philippines and the States. Through its pages, readers will embark on a journey that is as encouraging as it is empowering.

As you delve into this book, my prayer is that you will not only be inspired but that you will find hope in whatever situation you're facing. His courage to share his life's lessons and what God has done and continues to do in his life has been nothing short of inspirational and encouraging.

To my brother: Your talent and dedication have always inspired me, and I am so proud to see your dreams coming to fruition. May this book be the first of many, and may your words continue to touch and inspire all who read them.

Happy reading, and congratulations to my dear brother on this incredible achievement.

With love and admiration,
Dexter Quito
Husband, Girl Dad, Musician, REALTOR®, ABR®, SRS, PSA, GRI® at the Ashton RE/MAX Advantage in Nashville, TN.

ACKNOWLEDGMENTS

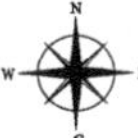

I am thankful for these people who have assisted me in fulfilling my dreams:

Rogelene Davis encouraged me to replace my air conditioning unit. She also helped me type all my journals in Microsoft Word.

Dexter Quito, my brother, encouraged me to continue writing and working on this book because I had already paid for an author coach. He told me not to change my mind even if others disagreed. He also taught me to write honestly in my journals and set goals. He even introduced me to the book *Leadership Pain* by Sam Chand.

Leo Quito, for continuous support as a brother and fellow United States Navy Sailor.

Samuel Chand, who introduced me to the Dream Releaser Publishing team. He encourages me to write because he believes everyone has a message the world is waiting to hear.

John Schondelmayer, Sarah Petelle, and Megan Adelson, for helping me finish the manuscript and the book itself.

Lieutenant Orpilla, Lieutenant Commander Stone, and Lieutenant Junior Grade Talisayon helped me submit my Medical Enlisted Commissioning Program (MECP) and mentored me while writing this book.

To the churches who welcomed me—in you, I have found real community and growth in my relationship with the Lord:

» Faith Family Fellowship in Cainta, Philippines.
» Northside Christian Church
» Berean Fundamental Baptist Church in Illinois.
» Lighthouse Church in Mount Juliet, TN
» ReGenesis Christian Church
» Five-Fold Church

INTRODUCTION

I was born and raised in Cainta Rizal, Philippines. My single mom raised me and my two older brothers. We were a middle-class family, but I always felt we had everything we needed due to my mom's love. My mom has always encouraged me to write journals and read books. To this very day, I still have that passion for journaling and reading. I was fourteen years old when my mom passed away in 1999. My brothers and I lived with my relatives in the Philippines, jumping from house to house. In 2003, after my high school years, my dad and stepmom petitioned us to come back to the US.

I was eighteen years old and new to this country. I found myself writing random topics that inspired me, like the fantastic scenery of nature, friendly people, and beautiful women. I can't believe I wrote over 300 pages worth of thoughts and feelings of inspiration. When I first arrived in the U.S., I felt sad because I missed my friends back in the Philippines, and I was full of regrets that I didn't ask the lady I liked to be my girlfriend. I was also still angry with my dad because he had left us and my mom. But I found that writing eased my sadness and regret. Writing something that inspires me gives me hope and joy.

The following year, in 2004, I got my driver's license. My dad encouraged me to join the United States Navy. It was a culture shock because my Recruit Division Commander (RDC) kept yelling at me, made me exercise, and woke me up very early. I didn't even have a debit card yet and didn't know how to use one. My journey into God's transformative power began during that painful time in boot camp. Like Charles Stanley says, "The dark moments of our lives will last only so long as is necessary for God to accomplish His purpose in us."[1] My broken relationship with my dad started to heal.

My first duty station was in San Diego, California, where I did three deployments and found myself writing my first official journal. When I moved to my second duty station here in Virginia in 2013, I found myself discouraged and sad again because of the church and friends I left in San Diego. So, in discouragement, I ripped up and threw out the first official journal. I asked myself, "Does God even want me to write a journal?" In 2014, I started writing and journaling again. I remember erasing everything I wrote, fearing that I might disobey God if I wrote. But that wrong belief began to change.

There are a few people I am grateful for who encouraged me to journal. First, my mom taught me the value of writing and reading. Second, my college instructor. I have five pages of an essay I needed to submit at that time. I asked my instructor how

I could become a better writer, and he told me to just keep on writing, but the only time I enjoyed writing was through journaling. So, I decided to develop my passion for journaling. You wouldn't be reading this book without my eldest brother, Dexter Quito, who encouraged me to write, journal, and set goals. I remember sharing my fear of journaling and setting goals with my brother. He told me that if you can't be honest with yourself through journaling, how could you be honest with others and the God who loves you? From then on, I poured myself into journaling, writing my deepest desires, failures, successes, secret sins, struggles, what I am thankful for, and what God was telling me.

Are you lonely and sad, looking for a way to find joy and fulfillment? Do you want to live life to the fullest and reach your full potential for God? Are you single and waiting for that special someone God has prepared for you? My friend, this book is for you. It is a compilation of my journal entries from 2014 to the present time—a ten-year period! I have become fully committed to journaling and writing again.

Before I started journaling, I was sad about my life and lacked motivation. Here are some benefits I have found in journaling that have healed the sadness:

1. Like I said earlier, writing something that inspires me gives me joy and hope. As soon as I pour myself into journaling, my sadness is gone, especially when I write what I am thankful for.
2. Journaling is a great way to revisit all the wonderful and fun experiences you have had with God.
3. Journaling helps you remember the promises of God in your life and how He has delivered you in incredible ways in the past. It helps your faith grow.
4. Journaling enables you to learn from your past! Document your past so that you don't waste what it can do for you now and in the future. Who knows, you may avoid making the same mistakes.
5. Journaling gives you a sense of purpose and a desire to live life to the fullest.
6. Journaling keeps you honest with yourself and authentic toward others and God.

You could convert your journal into a book—like I have—and share your message with others to help them with their walk. Everyone has a story, and the world is waiting to hear yours.

I invite you to read this book and, at the same time, journal what's in your heart. Reading this book teaches you about God's grace, the benefits of waiting, the value of obeying Him, and how to live an extraordinary life. This book is not a military book, although there are some stories about my experience in the US Navy. This book is not an autobiography, although it is replete with my emotional struggles, weaknesses, and successes. Instead, this book is a day-to-day devotional designed to grow you in your walk with God. This book is twenty-five years in the making, including all the lessons and experiences God taught me when I was a kid, dealing with the death of my mother. I pray that God fills you with joy, pleasure, wisdom, and satisfaction as you read this book.

"You will show me the path of life; In Your presence is fullness of joy; At Your right hand are pleasures forevermore."
—PSALM 16:11

DAY 1

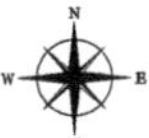

GRATITUDE IN HARDSHIP

Have you ever experienced heartbreak? When you're in it, it seems nobody knows its depth or can sympathize. Your body is longing for relief and comfort, or you are frantically searching for another love. Just remember that God knows this.

"Before I formed you in the womb I knew you; Before you were born I sanctified you."

—JEREMIAH 1:5

"Your eyes saw my substance, being yet unformed. And in Your book they all were written, The days fashioned for me, When as yet there were none of them."

—PSALM 139:16

When I was driving to Tennessee, I listened to God and worshiped Him. He showed me every detail of my past and His involvement. Now, I realize He was shaping my destiny, and His love for me is evident. His goodness overflowed within my heart during that drive:

- After living with my brothers without my mom, God brought us to the US to improve our living situation.
- God called me to boot camp to reshape and remove my anger toward my dad. I praise God for this; He brought me back home to redeem myself as I started to express my love and forgiveness.
- At age twenty-two, I joined the Navy and traveled to different countries. I can save money with God's help. Thank you, Lord.
- I can serve God in the local church and share His word with others in the Navy. It is such a privilege.
- I met Kelsey, my now ex-girlfriend, and experienced intimate love. I learned about relationships. I now appreciate life on a different level.

With all of this, tears flow from my eyes as I think about it. God's love and mercy fill my heart that a God of the universe weaves the story of my life into something beautiful. As Charles Stanley stated, "God has a plan for our lives. We are not accidents, nor do we exist by chance. Before we take our first breath, God knows how long we'll live" (See Psalm 13:16).[2] He knows our name long before we're born.

Before birth, God knew your life's stories from start to end.

As I started my drive to Chicago, I spoke with Pastor Barry. He told me the same thing I believed God was saying to me. My response is, "Lord, I want to know and experience Your love for me with all those beautiful things You've done in my life. I give You all glory, honor, and the highest praise."

If you're in the middle of heartbrokenness, remember how God showered you with mercy and goodness in the past. Before birth, God knew your life's stories from start to end. He loves you forever!

DAY 2

GOD FIGHTS YOUR BATTLES

Sometimes, God allows setbacks or failures to strengthen our faith and trust in Him. We appreciate Him more when we experience pain.

"Then all this assembly shall know that the Lord does not save with sword and spear; for the battle is the Lord's, and He will give you unto our hands."

—1 SAMUEL 17:47

Good morning Holy Spirit! First, I want to worship Jesus for His goodness. As I was studying for my test on Solid State Device, God told me that the battle was His, to go to bed early, and not to stress over the test. That night was the most restful sleep I have ever had before a test, so I had energy. I missed one item on the test, so that night, I studied again. I was nervous but not stressed or anxious. My coworker helps me learn too, so I am getting new information from him *and* from God.

I called my brothers and Sister Ellen to pray for me. Sister Ellen said that God put anointing in me, and whatever I touch will be blessed. If I want something, touch it, and I will have it. So, I touch the cars I want on my phone and claim it. I also touch the test paper before my tests start. During the test, I asked my instructor about troubleshooting, and she helped me explain it. Retaking the test taught me a lot, and I passed with flying colors—a score of 90 percent! I praise Jesus for the victory. I realized:

"And we know that all things work together for good to those who love God, to those who are the called according to His purpose."

—ROMANS 8:28

Failing it the first time prepares me for the next course and when I go to my ship. I see that the battle was for God, not for me. I am weak and nothing without Him. I give You all glory, honor, and praise, Lord.

I also passed the performance test; thank you, Jesus! This experience humbles me. He reminded me of His word in Psalm 60:12, "Through God, we will do valiantly."

Ultimately, God will give you victory and success because that's what He wants for you!

Setbacks put our courage and valiantness to the test. Through Christ, I experience victory and have done so bravely.

I pray that God gives you patience and wisdom through times of failure. Ask Him what He's trying to say to you during these times. Ultimately, God will give you victory and success because that's what He wants for you!

DAY 3

GOD BLESSES YOU WHEN YOU LEAST EXPECT IT

Have you ever been given gifts or shown extraordinary kindness from someone you didn't expect? Well, welcome to how God operates. He loves to surprise His faithful children with answers to their dreams and prayers in greater ways than they could ever expect.

"Now to Him who is able to do exceedingly abundantly above all that we ask or think, according to the power that works in us, to Him be glory in the church by Christ Jesus to all generations, forever and ever. Amen."

–EPHESIANS 3:20-21

God is about to present the lady. I can feel it. As I listen to the Holy Spirit, I am filled with certainty that He loves surprising His faithful children. I asked Him to remind me of the incredible things He has done for me. Then I realized when He gave me Kelsey, I had such a great time with her. I felt a love that I had never felt before from a woman. I experienced intimacy, and I am so grateful to God for that experience.

Another surprise blessing I received from God was when I graduated from Ships Surface Electrical Advanced Maintenance Course and was given forty days of leave I had plenty of time to pray, read, work out, write, sleep, and try delicious food. I was praying about where I was going after USS Ford. As I obeyed God, I experienced His best. As I picked my next order to transfer, I discovered it comes with two schools. Thank you, Jesus!

There are so many more things God has done for me, like making First Class Petty Officer and finding an apartment to get my basic allowance for housing. God gave me a place to live with a lovely family and a safe neighborhood right in front of Ms. Fe's house. The price was cheap, and I could save $40,000 by the time I left San Diego. When I came to Virginia, God provided me with a place to live with my brother Leo. So, I was able to save even more. As I obeyed, He provided all my needs. As Charles Stanley stated, "God loves to surprise His faithful people with answers to prayer far exceeding anything they had imagined."[3]

As I finish school, He's given me this theme:

"For the battle is the LORD's."

—1 SAMUEL 17:47

As I did a deep dive in Ephesians 3:20, God gave me more verses to help, bless, favor, and fight for me wherever I go—whether I'm at school, on the cruise ship, in different places like Hawaii, or with the love of my life. I am thinking on and praying about how God will surprise me with unexpected things. Amen!

"And Moses said to the people, 'Do not be afraid. Stand still, and see the salvation of the Lord, which He will accomplish for you today. For the Egyptians whom you see today, you shall see again no more forever. The LORD will fight for you, and you shall hold your peace.'"

—EXODUS 14:13-14

"And he said, 'Listen, all you of Judah and you inhabitants of Jerusalem, and you, King Jehoshaphat! Thus says the LORD to you: 'Do not be afraid nor dismayed because of this great multitude, for the battle is not yours, but God's."

—2 CHRONICLES 20:15

So, it's okay that I haven't met my girlfriend or future wife because God will provide her for me, respectfully fitted just for me—a beautiful, born-again Christian (and wealthy)! I will not hesitate to ask women for their names and numbers because God will present the lady and because He favors me. Amen!!

You can be full of hope.

From now on, begin your days, months, or even years with the strong faith that He is committed to your success and enjoyment because He has a plan for you. You can be full of hope.

DAY 4

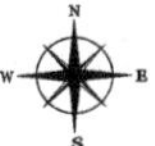

GOD IS GREATER THAN YOUR SIN

I am trying to figure out what is up with me. Every time I do something wrong, I feel sad and afraid. Are you the same way? Well, cheer up! Because today's devotion could change and free you from it.

I don't know what to write. I fell into lust last night. Instead of feeling guilty or sad today, the opposite happened as I asked for God's forgiveness. I felt such peace and joy that surpassed all understanding.

"If we confess our sins, He is faithful and just to forgive us our sins and to cleanse us from all unrighteousness."

—1 JOHN 1:9

The promise in this passage is that Jesus' sacrifice surpassed all our sins. No matter how far or deep we fall short, God's forgiveness and love are more significant than any sin we commit. Amen! When I disobeyed God by returning to Kelsey, my ex-girlfriend, God used Sister Ellen to bring me back to Him. Just as He promises me in Psalm 37:23-24, "The steps of a good man are ordered by the Lord, and He delights in his way. Though he falls, he shall not be utterly cast down; For the Lord upholds him with His hand."

As I repent, I can sense His love, favor, and goodness coming back to me. The Holy Spirit emphasizes that repentance turns God's wrath into favor from Him and from people.

As I go about my day, I have a sense of trust and peace in His faithfulness. In *Leadership Pain,* Sam Chand said, "Pain isn't an accident in God's world. Even when it's self-inflicted through doubt and sin, God graciously weaves the strands of these experiences into something beautiful—if we'll let Him."[4]

"Trust in the LORD with all your heart, and lean not on your own understanding. In all your ways acknowledge Him, and He shall direct your paths."

—PROVERBS 3:5-6

As I inquire of God, I trust His wisdom, love, and grace and am full of joy and peace. What is the way out of this situation? Out of lust? Then God gave me an incredible revelation from 2007 when I first struggled with lust. He freed me.

I sin, but His favor and love are greater. Indeed, God has done great things in my life.

I can serve God faithfully on the ship and traveling all over the world, and I can give thanks for my promotion to second class petty officer and my ability to save over $40,000. I sin, but His favor and love are greater. Indeed, God has done great things in my life. I returned to the Philippines twice and met my mentor, Chaplain Tar and Religious Petty Officer First Class Castillo.

2013: When I failed my C-school, I fell into lust, and here we go again—His love and forgiveness poured out of me. He uses me mightily at Northside Christian Church. The Holy Spirit introduced me to the community. God lifted me above my discouragement and opened my eyes to my true identity in Christ. Hallelujah! I was made first class petty officer. Glory to God. I got my associate degree in liberal arts. He performed healing miracles in my life. I don't wear glasses anymore. God has done a fantastic thing in my life. On December 2018, I met Kelsey, the first woman I ever loved.

2019: While dating Kelsey, I was tempted into viewing pornographic images online and e-books out of curiosity. Yet, no matter how shameful I felt confessing it, God's grace, favor, and love showered me. I don't deserve this, and God freely gave it to me. He makes Kelsey love and understand me even more. Her family is the same way, too.

As I open up to accept love and give love, my emotional life is healing little by little. Pastor Barry, my brothers Dexter and Leo, Mrs. Donna, Mr. Jeff, and Shauna have all loved and mentored me. I have learned the value of mentorship and how to be a good husband when my day comes.

I enjoyed dating Kelsey and the intimacy, both physical and emotional. As Dr. Henry Cloud says, "Our ability to give and respond to love is our greatest gift. The heart that God has fashioned in His image is the center of our being. Its ability to open up to love and allow love to flow outward is crucial to life. We need to claim our hearts as our property and work on our weaknesses. Doing so opens us up to life."[5]

2020: Rejection crept into my life because I was heartbroken. Kelsey and I broke up, but my relationship with God was the most intimate it had ever been during those times. The pain I had was unbearable, but God molded me. Rejection gave rise to lust, but God intervened again with the help of the Holy Spirit. The pain of rejection and brokenness can be healed through God's unfailing love.

"For his unfailing love for us is powerful; The LORD's faithfulness endures forever. Praise the LORD!"
—PSALM 117:2 (NLT)

His favor and love become greater and greater. Chaplain Kim counseled me with my break-up and struggle with lust. I opened up to him and felt relieved and understood. I finally transferred out of USS Ford and all my co-workers had lunch with me as a farewell. I felt satisfied with my time at Ford. The next thing I knew, God had something great in store. He sent me to two excellent C-schools: Electricians Mate Surface Ship Electrical Advance Maintenance and Electrical Component Maintenance Technician Air Pipeline (LHD-1). The drive from Virginia to Tennessee to Chicago was a fantastic road trip. God shows His faithfulness on those road trips when I listen. I also saw my beautiful niece and had a great time with my brother, his wife, Pastor Barry, and Mr. and Mrs. Atwood. It is nice to be back in Chicago. I've learned valuable lessons from my brother Dexter, and am so thankful to God for giving me a brother like him. He teaches me to be authentic in my journals and set goals.

Finally, I graduated from Electricians Mate Surface Ship Electrical Advance Maintenance. God helped me graduate from the challenging classes and thoroughly showed me His might. Thank you, Jesus! I give You all glory, honor, and praise because of Your goodness. He also let me stay in a lovely hotel by the beach. When I walked by the beach each afternoon, it felt like I was on vacation with thirty-eight days of leave. Hallelujah! In addition, every time I went to Tennessee, I felt the love of the people (Mrs. Donna, Pastor Barry, and my brother). Also, while staying in the hotel, God provided for all my needs, clothes, food, books, appliances, supplements, hobbies (PlayStation, guitar, mandolin), transportation, my plants, movies, friendship, and even a date.

"My God shall supply all your need according to His riches in glory by Christ Jesus."
—PHILIPPIANS 4:19

Why am I saying all of this? Because no matter what situation you are in right now, like my struggle with sin and disobedience, His forgiveness, love, blessing, grace, and favor are even greater than all we could imagine, ask, or think according to His power that works in us when we repent (See Ephesians 3:20). God loves to surprise his faithful children. Just TRUST in Him that He can graciously weave the strand of your life into something beautiful.

Like Dr. Don Colbert said, "From eternity's perspective, even big problems seem small."[6]

James also wrote, "You do not know what *will* happen tomorrow. For what *is* your life? It is even a vapor that appears for a little time and then vanishes away" (James 4:14).

> *"For I know the plans I have for you," declares the Lord, "plans to prosper you and not to harm you, plans to give you hope and a future."*
>
> —JEREMIAH 29:11 (NIV)

Like I said, Cheer up! God is in control. Breathe! Go to the beach and celebrate because no matter what you've done, God is more significant than your sin. His grace is bigger than all of it.

DAY 5

GOD WILL GIVE YOU THE DESIRES OF YOUR HEART

It's a great feeling to have your desires and dreams come true. Has that ever happened to you? You will experience many of those in your life because our Heavenly Father loves to grant the desires of your heart.

I'm asking God to give me one word, and He gave me Psalm 37:4.

"Delight yourself also in the Lord, and He shall give you the desire of your heart." So, I asked God if He wanted me to record all of the times He has been faithful in giving me the desires of my heart. The answer was, yes!

1990: As a kid, while playing outside, I saw a plane flying in the sky and started praying to God, "Lord, I want to ride a plane one day." Boarding a plane on the way to the US is like a dream come true.

1994: One day, I was looking at a magazine in the church and saw a spread for Disneyland. I told God I wanted to go there someday. The next thing I knew, my brother and I had the opportunity to visit, in addition to Universal Studios, Great America, and Bush Gardens. Thank You, Jesus.

"Now to him who is able to do exceedingly abundantly above all that we ask or think, according to the power that works in us."

—EPHESIANS 3:20

2015: He healed my eye! It's a miracle healing! I always wondered if I would have to wear glasses for the rest of my life. I got LASIK—for free! Thank you, Jesus! My eyes are much better now. All things are possible in Christ Jesus. I remember praying for God to heal my eyes so that I wouldn't have to wear glasses anymore because I spend $1,000 on them yearly. So, He did. I give You all glory, honor, and praise.

"Jesus said to him, 'If you can believe, all things are possible to him who believes.'"

—MARK 9:23

"But Jesus looked at them and said, 'With men it is impossible, but not with God; for with God; all things are possible.'"

—MARK 10:27

2020: When I was new in the Navy, I heard about the school Electricians Mate Surface Ship Electrical Advance Maintenance Course. A chief told me that I should go there because it is an excellent school, but I needed to figure out how. He told me to request it when I re-enlist or transfer. When I moved, I ended up at a different school but then flunked out. The failure prepared me to pass the Electricians Mate Surface Ship Electrical Advance Maintenance course. He reminded me that this school was my heart's desire before, and He granted it! Hallelujah! Thank you, Jesus!

Ask God to show you the dreams and desires He has granted in your life. Keep a journal of all the extraordinary things He has done. You will be amazed as He reveals it to you!

DAY 6

GOD WILL CARE FOR YOU

Isn't it nice when someone cares for you, thinks about you, and wants to be with you? Even better, provide all your needs, including housing, food, and allowances? This person could be your spouse, parents, siblings, or friends.

I listened to the song "Sparrow," by Cory Asbury, and God gave me this verse:

"When my father and my mother forsake me, Then the LORD will take care of me."

—PSALM 27:10

Throughout the years, God has been taking care of me. He has supplied all my needs, satisfied me with relationships, healed me, and protected me. He has given me grace, after grace, after grace.

God put Job 10:12 on my heart, "You have granted me life and favor, And Your care has preserved my spirit."

Sister Ellen told me the extraordinary favor of God is in me. He has given me life. She told me to read day 201 in the book *Promises*. There I learned that God provided me with eternal life, which can't be erased or changed.[7] I get to live in heaven forever—a house or place with my King. Not only has He given me eternal life, but He has also blessed me with an extraordinary life here on earth—a whole life. A rich and satisfying life.

He blesses me.

"I have come that they may have life, and that they may have it more abundantly."

—JOHN 10:10

"He who overcomes shall be clothed in white garments, and I will not blot out his name from the Book of Life; but I will confess his name before My Father and before His angels."

—REVELATION 3:5

Sister Ellen reminded me of Psalm 27:14, to wait for God's choice for my wife. I don't want the same marriage my mom had.

Last Friday, while lying in bed half asleep, I had lustful dreams. I repented, and God told me to trust Him! "Everything will be alright. I got your back." It is such a comfort that I don't have to think about my past sin or consequences because it only leads to guilt and fear. Instead, I get to enjoy the present moment of God's goodness and mercy.

"Trust in the LORD with all your heart, And lean not on your own understanding;
In all your ways acknowledge Him, And He shall direct your paths."
—PROVERBS 3:5-6

Blessed is the man who trusts in the Lord, And whose hope is the LORD. For he shall be like a tree planted by the waters, Which spreads out its roots by the river, And will not fear when heat comes; But its leaf will be green, And will not be anxious in the year of drought, Nor will cease from yielding fruit.
—JEREMIAH 17:7-8

He reminded me that He's been taking care of me all my years here on earth, so why wouldn't He care for me in my lowest valley or darkest hour? Why not in this very moment? Thank you, Lord.

As Don Colbert said, "Mindfulness works differently. It trains your mind to let go of any thought that is unrelated to the present moment and to find something to enjoy in the present continually."[8] God's Word echoes this sentiment:

"Therefore do not worry about tomorrow, for tomorrow will worry about its own things. Sufficient for the day is its own trouble."
—MATTHEW 6:34

Rejoice in the Lord always. Again I will say, rejoice! Let your gentleness be known to all men. The Lord is at hand. Be anxious for nothing, but in everything by prayer and supplication, with thanksgiving, let your requests be made known to God; and the peace of God, which surpasses all understanding, will guard your hearts and minds through Christ Jesus.
—PHILIPPIANS 4:4-7

Colbert added, "To have complete mental and physical health, mindfulness must become a way of life, a continual pattern for practicing relaxation during your day. Make mindfulness a habit by practicing it daily."[9]

Bless the Lord, O my soul;
And all that is within me, bless His holy name!
Bless the Lord, O my soul,
And forget not all His benefits:
Who forgives all your iniquities,
Who heals all your diseases,
Who redeems your life from destruction,
Who crowns you with lovingkindness and tender mercies,

Who satisfies your mouth with good things,
So that your youth is renewed like the eagle's.
—PSALM 103:1-5

Dr. Colbert stated:

It's interesting that the Bible says you enter His gates with thanksgiving because an attitude of gratitude helps you take the focus off your situation and shifts it to the One who can work everything out for you. Thankfulness and mindfulness will go a long way toward erasing the stress in your life.[10]

You will have similar benefits as you begin to live in the present moments instead of the past or future and as you give praise and thanksgiving to God every moment of every day.[11]

God has repeatedly given me the promises found in Lamentation 3:22-23: "*Through* the LORD's mercies we are not consumed, Because His compassions fail not. *They are* new every morning; Great *is* Your faithfulness."

Sister Ellen said, "God's faithfulness is new every morning. He is faithful to His promises. He is faithful to offer mercy, grace, forgiveness, and love." Amen!

If you are lonely—maybe you lost your parents, are single, have friends and relatives living in another state or country, remember Jesus! Our omnipotent and omnipresent God is more capable of caring for you than any human being you know. Stay in the present moment with Him. Rejoice and enjoy!

DAY 7

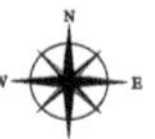

OBEY GOD

Have you ever asked yourself, "What's the use of following and obeying God?" The Bible is full of promises and stories of blessing for those who obey God.

Lord, thank you for your promises in Psalm 37:4, "Delight yourself also in the LORD, and He shall give you the desires of your heart."

I was so amazed when I looked back at something I wrote, just three simple words: "I am loved." God, the God of the universe, has performed miracles to give me the desires of my heart. I realize He is much more capable of providing than I ever could and has much more intimate knowledge of my heart's desires than I do. I got burned out in the Navy while I was at Ford. During this time, God told me through a friend to "always obey God. If God wants you to stay in the Navy, stay. If not, leave."

God knows what is best for us, and as we obey, God will bring excitement, adventure, blessing, and favor in every aspect of our lives. Looking back, as I waited on and followed Him, He blessed me tremendously and gave me rest for life, including while in the Navy. God put me in a position of authority in my shop as a leading petty officer and work center supervisor. In addition, God gave me favor when He sent me Kelsey, my now ex-girlfriend. I enjoyed that year with her. We've done incredible things together, like kayaking, visiting the Corvette Museum and Noah's Ark, and enjoying her family's company. On top of that, God sent me to two Navy enlisted classification schools for six months. It is such a rest and break for me. Hallelujah! Thank you, Jesus. Thoroughly, God has done exceedingly abundantly above all that I ask or think, above all my wildest dreams.

Now, God is asking me again to obey Him. Whether He wants me to get married or stay single, He will still give me favor, excitement, blessing, and adventure as I follow Him. Jesus knows what's best for me. He is more than capable of giving me the desires of my heart.

In *The Blessed Marriage*, authors Robert and Debbie Morris admonish readers to "trust God to meet those needs. He can take care of you far better than you can take care of yourself. He knows what you need more than you do."[12]

Lord, I will obey you! If you want me to be single, so be it. If you want me to be married, so be it. As I follow, I will trust in your promises in Ephesians 3:20 that You will do exceed our wildest dreams according to the power that works in us.

Lately, God has given me verses that excite me and fill me with joy.

Now it shall come to pass, if you diligently obey the voice of the LORD your God, to observe carefully all His commandments which I command you today, that the LORD your God will set you high above all nations of the earth. And all these blessings shall come upon you and overtake you, because you obey the voice of the LORD your God.

—DEUTERONOMY 28:1-2

When I was in Ford, He helped me pass all my Navy Maintenance and Material Management System inspections with flying colors—when I obeyed Him. Other electricians like EM2 Scribner, and Kavanah helped me tremendously, as well. In addition, my ex-girlfriend and I visited the Nashville Zoo, went paddle boating in Washington State, and ate at a restaurant I'd never been to. Your goodness made all this possible. I give you all joy, glory, honor, and praise.

We should not expect Him to always work in the same ways He has in the past but to expect the unexpected.

At the time, I found comfort in knowing that there are benefits to being single. If worst case scenario happened and Kelsey and me broke up (and we did later on), I would have all the freedom and energy in the world at all times. I could save my money, read the books I like, watch my favorite movies, date whomever I wanted, improve myself, serve God and worship Him more, listen to Him, pray whenever I want, eat whatever I want, go to school, travel, and sleep whenever I want. Thank you, Jesus, for the gift of singleness.

"Behold, I will do a new thing, Now it shall spring forth; Shall you not know it? I will even make a road in the wilderness And rivers in the desert."

—ISAIAH 43:19

God loves to work in our lives in new ways. We should not expect Him to always work in the same ways He has in the past but to expect the unexpected.

"Behold, the former things have come to pass, And new things I declare; Before they spring forth I tell you of them."

—Isaiah 42:9

We often expect the Lord to act in a certain way, but God often has a plan that we know nothing about. Although the people of Israel expected the Messiah to come as a great warrior as David had been, God had a different plan. This would lead to the salvation of all who believe in Him. Never underestimate His ability to rectify a situation. Rather, trust Him and obey His wonderful will.[13]

—Dr. Charles Stanley

"And keep the charge of the LORD your God: to walk in His ways, to keep His statutes, His commandments, His judgments, and His testimonies, as it is written in the Law of Moses, that you may prosper in all that you do and wherever you turn."

—King 2:3

As David drew close to death, he passed on the most important principle of his life to his son, Solomon—obey God. Nothing is more important for us to teach our children and encourage those around us than to submit to the Lord, walk in His ways, and trust His mighty hand (Hebrews 3:13). Through obedience, we know Him and enjoy His marvelous blessings (Psalm 103).[14]

—Dr. Charles Stanley

"Eye has not seen, nor ear heard, Nor have entered into the heart of man The things which God has prepared for those who love Him."

—1 Corinthians 2:9

We have no idea all that God wants to do in and through us. In our limited understanding, we have yet to imagine what is possible for us the intimacy with the Lord, power, freedom, spiritual blessings, and peace that belong to us when we become His children (Ephesians 1). But God who is perfect in His knowledge and wisdom does, and His Holy Spirit, who indwells us from the moment of our salvation, reveals the depths of His purpose and plan to us through His word when we seek Him.[15]

—Dr. Charles Stanley

"Everyone who is called by My name, Whom I have created for My glory; I have formed him; yes, I have made him."

—Isaiah 43:7

"Do you realize that the God of heaven has created you for His glory? He wants the world to see some of His majesty and goodness through you, and He wants to crown you with His own splendor."[16]

—Dr. Charles Stanley

Now it shall come to pass, if you diligently obey the voice of the LORD your God, to observe carefully all His commandments which I command you today, that the LORD your God will set you high above all nations of the earth. And all these blessings shall come upon you and overtake you because you obey the voice of the LORD your God: Blessed shall you be in the city, and blessed shall you be in the country. Blessed shall be the fruit of your body, the produce of your ground and the increase of your herds, the increase of your cattle and the offspring of your flocks. Blessed shall be your basket and your kneading bowl. Blessed shall you be when you come in, and blessed shall you be when you go out.

—DEUTERONOMY 28:1-6

"Your ears shall hear a word behind you, saying, 'This is the way, walk in it,' Whenever you turn to the right hand Or whenever you turn to the left."

—ISAIAH 30:21

Though I'd read these verses before, I felt God gave me new revelation this time. I asked God why He didn't exceed my expectations with my crush, Olivia. God assured me that He is about to do wonders and answer prayers that would exceed my expectations. He said He would fulfill His promises to me in a manner better than all I have written, dreamed, or envisioned in my journal. I should not underestimate His power to redeem or rectify every aspect of my life, including my love, spiritual, emotional, and work life. Hallelujah! Thank You, Jesus! Just obey closely, like David reminds Solomon in 1 Kings 2:3. It is about to happen.

The next time God tells you to do something, don't hesitate.

Lord, open my spiritual ears so I can hear You guiding me. Open my spiritual eyes to see what You are about to do. Holy Spirit, always gives me a passion for obeying God no matter what.

Now therefore, if you will indeed obey My voice and keep My covenant, then you shall be a special treasure to Me above all people; for all the earth is Mine.

—EXODUS 19:5

The next time God tells you to do something, don't hesitate. Prioritize obedience to Him. It will put you in a favorable position before Him and man.

DAY 8

THERE'S TREASURE IN THE WAITING

Our society associates waiting with negative things like passivity, laziness, and unproductiveness. Our culture encourages the now and fast way of living. However, it takes discernment to know when and when not to wait. The Bible promises excellent rewards to those who wait. God never sleeps! Have you heard tragic stories of people who messed up their lives because they didn't wait? Do you have personal stories of a great reward because you waited?

Do you not know? Have you not heard? The LORD is the everlasting God, the Creator of the ends of the earth. He will not grow tired or weary, and his understanding no one can fathom. He gives strength to the weary and increases the power of the weak. Even youths grow tired and weary, and young men stumble and fall; but those who hope in the LORD will renew their strength. They will soar on wings like eagles; they will run and not grow weary, they will walk and not be faint.

—ISAIAH 40:28-31 (NIV)

Lately, I've become weary of my singlehood. My whole body craves to be loved and emotionally satisfied. It took twelve years before God gave me a girlfriend. So, I thought about what God taught me during those years of waiting:

1. I learned to choose my friends carefully.
2. God freed me from lust through grace.
3. I've learned how to handle money.
4. I've learned to take care of my body.
5. I've learned what I need as an introvert.
6. I've learned my true identity in Christ.
7. I've learned to claim God's favor and promises.
8. I've learned that obedience always leads to blessing.
9. I've reaped more than what I've sown and later than I had expected.
10. God opened up opportunities for me to serve Him, travel worldwide, and finish my associate's degree.

11. God redeemed me and fixed my relationship with my dad.
12. I've learned to set boundaries.
13. God brought back my interest in leading.
14. I've learned about relationships.

These lessons are priceless and worth the wait. I love You, and thank you, Jesus. I give You all glory, honor, wisdom, and praise.

Reflecting on this list, I'm amazed at what God has done in my life. Now I know I'm not wasting this season of singleness while I wait for a girlfriend. As Pastor Hunk said in his sermon, "Sometimes God's got to get you ready for the thing He's getting ready to do, for something amazing in your life." Hallelujah!

Through my impatience and weariness about founding a girlfriend or my wife, God reminded me of the time I was burned out in the Navy while working on the USS Ford ship. The only cure for stress and discouragement when nothing is happening is waiting on the Lord. As Jesus promises to renew my strength, I shall "mount up with wings like eagles; I shall run and not be weary; I shall walk and not faint" (Isaiah 40:31). In addition, when I obeyed God in whatever He wanted, He rekindled the enthusiasm for my job in the Navy. I led fifteen people as a work center supervisor and leading petty officer. God and man showed me such favor and high esteem. Thank you, Jesus. You work in mysterious ways.

The same applies to every aspect of my life, including my love life. As I wait on the Lord, He renews my strength. I shall run and not be weary; I shall walk and not faint. As I obey Him, He will rekindle my life, including my love life, with excitement and adventure.

He comforted me with Isaiah 64:4: "For since the beginning of the world Men have not heard nor perceived by the ear, nor has the eye seen any God besides You, Who acts for the one who waits for Him."

I believe that waiting involves listening to God's directions.

God also reminded me that I will graduate and finish my electrical component maintenance technician air pipeline course because He promised it.

"Through God we will do valiantly, for it is He who shall tread down our enemies."

—PSALM 60:12

"So whatever the LORD our God takes possession of before us, we will possess."
—JUDGES 11:24

"For the battle is the LORD's, and He will give you into our hands."
—1 SAMUEL 17:47

He also promised that my mutual fund would grow to one million. Thank you, Jesus! I give you all glory, honor, praise, wealth, and riches.

I believe that waiting involves listening to God's directions. Don't be discouraged when you feel like you've been waiting on God to give you something you've been praying for. He never sleeps! When you wait on Him for something, you allow Him to provide the best experiences and the best of everything. You will be amazed and glad that you waited.

DAY 9

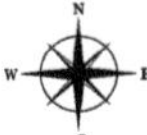

CHRIST WILL DELIVER YOU

Do you know that you can do anything and achieve the extraordinary? The Bible is full of promises and encouraging words that you can reach your dreams, desires, and goals. His GRACE makes it all possible; all you have to do is have FAITH.

I was in bed last night, about to sleep, when God spoke to me in a mighty way. He truly opened the eyes of my understanding. Here's what I heard:

1. All things are possible through Christ (See Mark 10:27).
2. I am always victorious (See 2 Corinthians 2:14).
3. He will deliver me from ALL my troubles (See Psalm 53:7).
4. All things are possible to those who believe (See Mark 9:23).
5. I can do all things through Christ (See Philippians 4:13). What great news! I can finish my thirty years in the Navy. I can be a millionaire and retire in the Navy for twenty or thirty years in service. Hallelujah! I give You all glory, honor, and praise.

"Many are the afflictions of the righteous, But the LORD delivers him out of them all."

—PSALM 34:19

I encourage you to dream big and set high goals. First, write what you really, really want. Second, figure out your priorities. Third, ask yourself, what are your greatest dreams, since everything is possible through Christ? Fourth, create a goal to achieve that dream. As the saying goes, "The sky is the limit." God's grace is infinite.

DAY 10

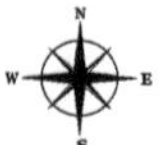

ENJOY HIM

Think about this: If everything belongs to God—your dreams, satisfaction, family, and enjoyment—doesn't it make sense to give total allegiance to God, too? His best plan for your life will manifest when you surrender all you have and are to Him. You can't go wrong.

"Every good gift and every perfect gift is from above, and comes down from the Father of lights, with whom there is no variation or shadow of turning."

—JAMES 1:16

First of all, I want to thank God for James 1:16. All good and perfect gift comes from Him. Every enjoyable and pleasurable moment that happens to us is a gift from God. Walking in His ways and obeying Him are vital. As John Bevere said, "There is nothing good for you outside the will of God."[17]

"Teach those who are rich in this world not to be proud and not to trust in their money, which is so unreliable. Their trust should be in God, who richly gives us all we need for our enjoyment."

—1 TIMOTHY 6:17 (NLT)

Prayer:

Thank you, Father, for the many blessings, extraordinary favor, protection, joy, great satisfaction, pleasure, and enjoyment You've showered over my life. I give You all praises, the highest honor, glory, power, wisdom, knowledge, riches, wealth, authority, leadership, beauty, gifts, and talent. I surrender my will and everything to You.

Watch how powerfully He will move in your life. You will never be the same again!

Tell God daily, "I surrender all I am and have to you." Watch how powerfully He will move in your life. You will never be the same again!

DAY 11

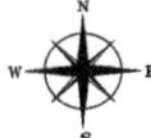

EXPECT SOMETHING GREATER

There are times you'll end up in situations you don't want to be in. You want a way out because it's scary and requires hard work. God wants you to stay in these trials because He knows that great rewards and benefits will follow.

"I have come that they may have life, and that they may have it more abundantly."

—JOHN 10:10

There are numerous verses about the blessings that come from waiting on God. God wants me to stay in my current position in the mess desk. It's a complicated position and requires a lot of leadership. I watched the ocean and heard God's still small voice. He comforted me that this assignment is only temporary; soon enough, He will place me into His hands of blessing and favor. He reminded me that I am meant for more—an excellent, whole life. His purpose is to give me a rich and satisfying life at its fullest.

Take courage on the promises of God because He is faithful.

"For since the beginning of the world Men have not heard nor perceived by the ear, Nor has the eye seen any God besides You, Who acts for the one who waits for Him."

—ISAIAH 64:4

But those who wait on the Lord Shall renew their strength; They shall mount up with wings like eagles, They shall run and not be weary, They shall walk and not faint.

—ISAIAH 40:31

"The LORD is good to those who wait for Him, To the soul who seeks Him."

—LAMENTATIONS 3:25

God also encouraged me that all my goals for this year will be fulfilled.

Take courage on the promises of God because He is faithful. Talk to a trusted friend, ask for help, make sure you get enough sleep, walk to the beach, and do things that could relieve your stress. Most importantly, ask God to comfort you because, in Him, we find solace.

DAY 12

THROUGH THE LORD'S MERCIES

Simply look at the miraculous things God has done for you in your past, and you will want nothing more than to rejoice. Try it! Ask Him to show you the great and mighty things He has done in your life. You will be amazed at what He is willing to show you.

"Through the Lord's mercies we are not consumed, Because His compassions fail not. They are new every morning; Great is Your faithfulness."

—LAMENTATIONS 3:22-23

"And we know that all things work together for good to those who love God, to those who are the called according to His purpose."

—ROMANS 8:28

I asked God why I am in the supply department and the Navy. I prayed for Him to show me great and mighty things I did not know. Then, as I listened, my heart and mind were filled with gratitude for Him.

Every day, write what you're thankful for.

» Thank you, God, for placing me in the supply department instead of as a petty officer of the watch in cold weather in the duty section.

» Thank you, Jesus. Because of my stable income, I can visit and take a vacation. In fact, the income is far more than what I need, but it has allowed me to revisit San Diego, La Jolla Cove, Disneyland, Universal Studios, and SeaWorld and taste different Filipino food.

» God gave me the pleasure of visiting Mr. and Mrs. Wardrobe, my old church in San Diego, Yosemite, San Francisco, Opry Land Hotel, Mammoth Cave, Rock

City, the White House, the Smithsonian Museum, the Air and Space Museum, New York, Williamsburg, and the Golden Gate Bridge.

» Thank you, Father. Because of the Navy, I have the privilege to serve You in the church.
» Thank you, Jesus, for giving me a stable job and income. I can buy the food I want and nice clothes and books, watch incredible movies (like Marvel!), and listen to my favorite music. You meet my daily needs.
» Thank you, Father, that I am still alive and well when I almost drowned in Wawa River in the Philippines. It is only by Your Mercy and compassion that I get to experience the beauty of Your creation.

Go buy a journal. Every day, write what you're thankful for. Every day, your countenance will be full of zest to live another day. Loneliness will have no room in you. Trust me!

DAY 13

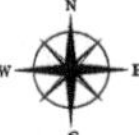

HE FREELY GIVES YOU ALL GOOD THINGS

Have you ever written down a goal or a dream? It's a wise thing to do. I encourage you to dream big and set audacious goals that you like, different from what other people want. The God of heaven and earth is more than capable of making it happen. There is also a science behind thinking big—it gives you more vigor to accomplish extraordinary dreams. You'll have a more positive view of life because mediocrity is not in your dictionary.

"He who did not spare His own Son, but delivered Him up for us all,
how shall He not with Him also freely give us all things?"
—ROMANS 8:32

God reminded me while sitting on my rack bed that He had given me everything. His purpose is to provide us with "a rich and satisfying life" (John 10:10, NLT). His goodness and mercy have followed me all the days of my life.

Jesus died for you on the cross so that you would have an abundant, extraordinary, and prosperous life.

On December 17, 2018, He promised me that every goal I wrote down in 2017 would be accomplished:

1. Receive a brand new and obedient heart for Him.
2. Stay healthy. To live in divine health.
3. Expect one billion dollars and receive it.
4. Write a book about the grace and goodness of Jesus Christ.

5. Finish my bachelor's in health care management and nursing, become a certified pastor, and be an officer in the Navy.
6. Learn how to play and excel in keyboard, mandolin, banjo, guitar, and violin.
7. Meet my girlfriend who will one day become my wife, beautiful and wealthy, and beyond my dreams and expectations (See Ephesians 3:20).
8. Enjoy traveling and visiting Jerusalem (where Jesus was born), Mount Mayon in the Philippines, Niagara Falls in Canada, Banaue Rice Terraces, Japan, Finland, Sweden, Greenland, Venezuela, France, Spain, Tower of Pisa in Italy, England, New Zealand, the Red Sea where Jesus walked..
9. Finish twelve books (See Appendix for a complete list of books that have influenced my life).

Don't fear what others think of you as you work towards big dreams and goals. Jesus died for you on the cross so that you would have an abundant, extraordinary, and prosperous life. Trust Jesus because you're fulfilling the remarkable life He desires for you.

DAY 14

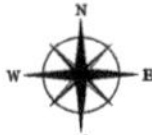

HE WILL REIGN IN YOUR LIFE

Those of us who have accepted Jesus Christ as our Savior have a significant advantage over those who don't. The Holy Spirit lives in us, and His unlimited grace (empowerment) is available. You may notice the favor and blessing in disguise, whether in your career, finances, health, or relationship.

"For if by the one man's offense death reigned through the one, much more those who receive abundance of grace and of the gift of righteousness will reign in life through the One, Jesus Christ."
—ROMANS 5:17

I was praying in my room, believing and asking God to show me the great and mighty things He has done for me. Then, He showed me Romans 5:17. Since I joined the Navy, God has shown me His grace and favor for success. In ACU–1, He enabled me to travel worldwide and make good friends. Through His favor, I made a second-class petty officer, which advanced me exponentially. Then, I moved to Mid-Atlantic Regional Maintenance Center (MARMC) in Norfolk, Virginia.

You're destined to reign in this life.

God taught me about biblical finance and led me to counsel numerous sailors, which I really enjoyed. While there, I found favor from my leaders, who gave me an early promotion three times. As a result, I became a first-class petty officer at my new command (USS Ford). I love this command; it feels like I am still on shore duty. Thank you, Jesus, that You made me the head and not the tail; I shall be above only and not beneath (See Deuteronomy 28:13). You are thoroughly faithful to your promises.

Be confident! You're destined to reign in this life, ten times much better than your counterpart. Like Daniel, who was distinguished ten times better because of his excellent spirit! (see Daniel 1:20)

DAY 15

HE IS FAITHFUL TO THE END

When was the last time you had to make a difficult decision? Difficult decisions can make us nervous and tense because one wrong move could change the trajectory of our lives. But it doesn't need to be that way because the wisest and most potent Being—the Holy Spirit—is living in us and will never leave nor forsake us. Utilize Him and listen for His guidance.

"Through the LORD's mercies we are not consumed, Because His compassions fail not. They are new every morning; Great is Your faithfulness."
—LAMENTATIONS 3:22-23

I needed a new car but was nervous about spending my emergency fund. I was left with $2,000. At the same time, praise the Lord because I have a new car—a 2013 Honda Civic EX, which is fully paid for. God answered my question about when to buy the car—the time was now! Thank God!

The Holy Spirit guided me to the right car. I praise God for giving me the desires of my heart. Thorough obedience leads to blessing. As Charles Stanley says, "If the Lord is bringing something to your mind right now, consider this: It could be that you have been living in the same uncomfortable situation for years because at some point, you chose to do things your way instead of God's way."[18]

I have been driving my old car too long, and it's always under repair. God gave me wisdom and direction in buying my second car. Thank you, Lord! He assured me of His faithfulness, that He will build my emergency fund again, but this time, much greater. He reminds me of the song I composed, "Faithful to the End," when I was twenty years old and new in the Navy and the US. My heart just cried as I worshiped Him and His faithfulness.

Lord, You're faithful; You're loving; You're good.
Lord, You're faithful; You're loving; You're good.
You have a plan for me.
You have a plan for me.
So, we sing Hallelujah.

So, we sing Hallelujah.
So, we sing Hallelujah.
So, we sing Hallelujah.
Lord, You're faithful and faithful to the end.

Spend some time and bring your concerns and big decisions you have to make to the Holy Spirit. Spend some time listening to Him. Do exactly and wholeheartedly what He wants.

DAY 16

THE GREAT HIGH PRIEST

Do you ever feel like the God of this Universe doesn't care about the details of your life? God encourages us to ask Him ordinary questions. He is so vast that He might wait to answer you, but He sympathizes with you in all things, just like a loving parent would.

Seeing then that we have a great High Priest who has passed through the heavens, Jesus the Son of God, let us hold fast our confession. For we do not have a High Priest who cannot sympathize with our weaknesses, but was in all points tempted as we are, yet without sin. Let us therefore come boldly to the throne of grace, that we may obtain mercy and find grace to help in time of need.

—HEBREWS 4:14-16

Yesterday, God spoke to me and told me He is my Defender, Comforter, High Priest, Compassionate Friend, and Merciful Companion, that I could come to Him boldly with whatever I feel or think. He will accept me and love me. He is not shocked by my weaknesses and failures when I am afraid and confused. He will help and extend His mercy and grace over my life.

You will be amazed at the comfort He will bring you.

I encourage you to listen to the song "Before the Throne of God Above" by Shane and Shane. You will feel blessed by it. In fact, you could tell Jesus Christ the very feeling you have right now, whether you are sad, lonely, happy, or confused. You will be amazed at the comfort He will bring you.

DAY 17

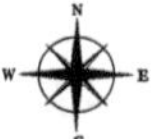

YOU ARE REDEEMED

What was your life like before you met Jesus Christ? Once you accept Jesus Christ as your Savior, you are a blessed, favored, anointed, prosperous, and forgiven child of God. Continue declaring it and claiming those promises because they are right and true.

WordReference.com[19] yielded many definitions for the word "redeemed" including:

» To obtain the release or restoration of, as from captivity, by paying ransom.
» To discharge or fulfill (a pledge, promise)
» To recover by payment or other satisfaction
» To buy back or pay off; clear by payment: to redeem a mortgage.
» To exchange (bonds, trading, stamps) for money or goods

This fourth of July, our declaration of Independence from the British colony reminds me of our freedom and the gift of abundant life through His Son, Jesus Christ. Just like the definition of redemption, Jesus Christ reclaims, recovers, wins, and exchanges His life so that we can have eternal life in Him.

On a personal note, back in 2006, after I broke up with my girlfriend Cecile, I was addicted to lust and led astray from the will of God. I lost respect, favor, my savings, my civilian job, and the blessings of God.

Today, God reminds me of His wonderful promises in Psalms 103:2-5:

Bless the LORD, O my soul,
And forget not all His benefits:
Who forgives all your iniquities,
Who heals all your diseases,
Who redeems your life from destruction,
Who crowns you with lovingkindness and tender mercies,
Who satisfies your mouth with good things,
So that your youth is renewed like the eagle's.

Now, it's July 4, 2018! It's been twelve years since that feeling of loss. God indeed recovered and REDEEMED what the devil had stolen. God blessed me mightily. He has showered me with extraordinary favor. I tell myself, "I am more than a conqueror who walks in the extraordinary favor of God and man."

Since then, He has given me wealth ($100,000 in savings), a good reputation, a stable job and income, joy, honor, love, divine health, respect, faithful friends, promotion, and a solid church home. Thank you, Father God, for the talent and ministry and for using me mightily for Your glory. I praise You, Jesus, for giving me a blessed memory, a high-class lifestyle, valuable books, exciting movies, and a gym membership.

If you have not accepted Jesus Christ as your personal Savior, I invite you to pray this prayer:

"Jesus, I want to be part of your family. Forgive me for all my sins. I invite you to live in me and be my personal Savior. Thank you for dying for me on the Cross. You gave Your life so that I can have an abundant life. In Jesus' name, I pray, Amen!"

DAY 18

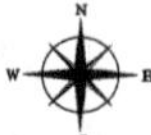

FAITHFULNESS THROUGH THE YEARS

You have probably asked God before about things you don't understand. You may or may not get the answer you want, but He will do anything to reveal His will in your life. You need to create time to listen to Him and be willing to obey whatever He tells you to do.

Your most significant success will come from the Holy Spirit's straightforward instruction, and your greatest blessing could come from the smallest acts of obedience.

Thank you, Jesus, for these verses:

"Call to Me, and I will answer you, and show you great and mighty things, which you do not know."
—JEREMIAH 33:3

"I will instruct you and teach you in the way you should go; I will guide you with My eye."
—PSALM 32:8

"Your ears shall hear a word behind you, saying, 'This is the way, walk in it,' Whenever you turn to the right hand Or whenever you turn to the left."
—ISAIAH 30:21

Through these years, God reminds me that I have prosperity only because of His guidance, counsel, and instruction. It's been ten years since I joined the Navy, and I have seen God's power, wisdom, protection, mercy, and grace. He is faithful to do it again and again. It's been thirty years since I was born, and I have seen God's sovereignty, faithfulness, and compassion for me. You are my everything, Jesus.

Your most significant success will come from the Holy Spirit's straightforward instruction, and your greatest blessing could come from the smallest acts of obedience. Listen to Him!

DAY 19

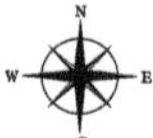

THE REST, SATISFACTION, AND PLEASURE YOU DESIRE

Did you know God can give you the pleasure and satisfaction you crave? He created human beings, and He knows exactly how to fulfill your desires and wants.

"You will show me the path of life; In Your presence is fullness of joy; At Your right hand are pleasures forevermore."
—PSALM 16:11

"The fear of the LORD leads to life, And he who has it will abide in satisfaction; He will not be visited with evil."
—PROVERBS 19:23

I praise You, Lord Jesus, for a "more-than-enough" kind of life.

God has thoroughly granted me rest, joy, pleasure, and satisfaction that can be found only in Him. As I look back, I see that God has given me rest in all realms of my life and the world around me. Thank you, Jesus. I praise You, Lord Jesus, for a "more-than-enough" kind of life, a life abounding with extraordinary favor and blessings.

Claim His promises in Psalms 16:11 and Proverbs 19:23, and speak them loudly over your life.

DAY 20

HIS GREAT GRACE

You may think you know everything about yourself: your strengths, weaknesses, achievements, etc. But God, whose mind is infinite, gave you and me a grace that empowers us to do the extraordinary and beyond.

"And God is able to make all grace abound toward you, that you, always having all sufficiency in all things, may have an abundance for every good work."
—2 CORINTHIANS 9:8

Thank you, Jesus, for your Word and for great grace, that you, oh God, make all grace abound toward me in every area of my life.

I have total and complete sufficiency in every area of my life at all times.

"Blessed be the God and Father of our Lord Jesus Christ, who has blessed us with every spiritual blessing in the heavenly places in Christ."
—EPHESIANS 1:3

"And He said to me, 'My grace is sufficient for you, for My strength is made perfect in weakness.' Therefore most gladly I will rather boast in my infirmities, that the power of Christ may rest upon me."
—2 CORINTHIANS 12:9

According to John Bevere's book *Extraordinary*:

» Grace gives (me) the ability to go beyond (my) own ability in every area of my life to please God to live extraordinarily. [20]

» Grace empowers us beyond our ability. This is why it is extraordinary.[21]

» Grace gives me the power to go beyond my own natural ability. It brings me into the extraordinary realm.[22]

» Grace is God's free gift that forgives, saves, recreates, and empowers us to live a holy life. It also enables us to advance the kingdom by going beyond our ability. Just as grace saves us from eternal death, it empowers us to live extraordinarily in all means of life.[23]

» Grace has been freely given to me, so I can now do what would otherwise be impossible. I can go beyond my human ability to accomplish the extraordinary because of His grace—all to His glory.[24]

Be open to what God can do in your life.

Don't limit yourself to your past mistakes or others' negative words about you. Be open to what God can do in your life. Believe and have faith because faith is the key to accessing His grace to live the life you are meant to live.

DAY 21

THE LIFE ABUNDANT

I can't emphasize enough the magnitude of what Jesus Christ has done for you on the cross, both spiritually and physically. Because of His sacrifice, you have eternal life in heaven and abundant life here. Aware or unaware, He moves in our lives for our benefit and to care for us.

"I have come that they may have life, and that they may have it more abundantly."

—JOHN 10:10

As I stand in the kitchen at home, looking inside the refrigerator, on the table, in the food cabinet, and on top of the freezer, all I see are delicious and healthy foods. God's abundance has overwhelmed me. I never had such high-quality food back in the Philippines. He gave me these verses:

"The young lions lack and suffer hunger; But those who
seek the Lord shall not lack any good thing."

—PSALM 34:10

"For the LORD God is a sun and shield; The LORD will give grace and glory;
No good thing will He withhold From those who walk uprightly."

—PSALMS 84:11

"And my God shall supply all your need according to His riches in glory by
Christ Jesus. Now to our God and Father be glory forever and ever. Amen."

—PHILIPPIANS 4:19-20

God thoroughly supplies all my needs—not some—but *all* of them. My needs have all been met and satisfied. Thank you, Jesus! He has lavishly showered me with the best things.

Take some time to give thanks for all the
beautiful things He has done for you.

In closing, James Robinson said this in an endorsement of John Bevere's book *Extraordinary*:

John Bevere is one of the most passionate people I know, and I believe he has truly grasped the meaning of John 10:10: "I came that they may have life and have it abundantly." In Extraordinary, he digs into the word to show what it looks like to please God and use the talents He has given us. John pushes believers to the edge to get them to launch out into the deep. He lives life to the fullest and, through these pages, will inspire you to experience the joy of serving Christ with passion.[25]

This is how we should be living, too.

Take some time to give thanks for all the beautiful things He has done for you. Write them down and meditate on them.

DAY 22

A VERY PRESENT HELP

Has your friend ever told you to relax, breathe, and calm down? Have you ever been frightened only to find out everything was okay? In those times, God says, "relax, breathe, and calm down because I am here to help you." Isn't that reassuring?

"God is our refuge and strength, A very present help in trouble."

–PSALM 46:1

"Fear not, for I am with you; Be not dismayed, for I am your God. I will strengthen you, Yes, I will help you, I will uphold you with My righteous right hand."

–ISAIAH 41:10

Thank God for these verses. He gave these to me two weeks ago when my chief asked me to go on Temporary Assigned Duty (TAD) in a cargo/elevator shop. I was alarmed and didn't know what to say until I remembered what God told me. He wanted me to relax, trust Him, and have peace and joy because He would be with me to prosper me. He would strengthen, help, and uphold me. As it turns out, I did not end up at cargo/elevator. Thank God for it.

Gratitude and claiming God's promises are bulletproof ways to calm your heart and mind.

Gratitude and claiming God's promises are bulletproof ways to calm your heart and mind. A fireman made fun of me, calling me racial names while everyone listened, but I prayed Psalms 46:1 over the situation. It soothed my mind, and I began to sing His praises:

- I praise Him for the courage and opportunity He gave me to confront the fireman and tell him that his remarks offended me and hurt me. He stopped picking on me.
- I praise You, Jesus, for the opportunity to teach my co-worker Gonzales how to use spiritual warfare through prayer. She was my co-worker on the USS Ford ship; Gonzales sharpened me, too, and reminded me of Romans 1:16, "For I am not ashamed of the gospel of Christ, for it is the power of God to salvation for everyone who believes."
- Thank you, Jesus, for sending people to encourage me, like Tim, Isaac, Tyler, Gonzales, Interior Communication First Class Diaz, and the Electrician's Mate Chief Petty Officer McFadden.
- Thank you, Jesus, for using my supervisor to counsel me on how to confront the fireman.
- Thank you, Jesus, for protecting my reputation in my branch, Visual Landing Aid (VLA).
- I praise You. Through your strength, I can show grace and forgiveness to the fireman.
- Thank You, Jesus. I can show grace to my friend and help her get home when she needs a ride.
- I praise You, Jesus, for not sending me to deployment. Indeed, You are my refuge and strength, a very present help in trouble. Indeed, those who trust in You will never be put to shame.
- Thank You, Jesus! I can take college classes now that I'm not deploying.
- Do you feel afraid of the unknown or guilty because of some mistakes? Pray and claim the promises of God in Psalm 46:1 and Isaiah 41:10 because Jesus Christ is a compassionate God.

DAY 23

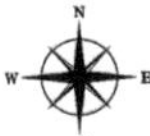

FORGET NOT ALL HIS BENEFITS

Today, I'm thinking about this verse in Psalm 103: 1-5. The writer, King David, is counting the many blessings God has given him. Even a thousand years ago, people experienced gratitude and see the manifestation of God's goodness. How has God benefitted you as a child of God?

Bless the LORD, O my soul;
And all that is within me, bless His holy name!
Bless the LORD, O my soul,
And forget not all His benefits:
Who forgives all your iniquities,
Who heals all your diseases,
Who redeems your life from destruction,
Who crowns you with lovingkindness and
tender mercies,
Who satisfies your mouth with good things,
So that your youth is renewed like the eagle's.
—PSALM 103:1-5

You are King of Kings; I bow before you, Lord of Lords.

Lord, I worship you, Jesus! I magnify your name. I exalt you. I lift your name on high. You are King of Kings; I bow before you, Lord of Lords. I praise your mighty name; you are Jehovah Jireh, my provider, Lord; you shower me with benefits and blessings. I will never grow tired of counting them.

- » You heal all my pains and aches.
- » You forgive me forever and declare me righteous through Christ.

» You redeem and lead me away from destruction and ruin of lust, poor boundaries, and bad friends.
» You crown me with loving kindness, extraordinary favor, caring friends, and a loving church family.
» Thank you, Jesus, for redeeming me and giving me the Holy Spirit for guidance.
» You satisfy and give me pleasure and joy from all the good things You've given me.
» You have given me exceedingly great and precious promises.

Thank you, Jesus, for all the benefits of life with you, Jesus! I can never outgive You.
Meditate on Psalms 103:1-5, and reflect on these questions:

1. What bad thing have you done that God has already forgiven?
2. What acute condition did God heal you from?
3. What were the darkest and scariest years of your life that God redeemed you from?
4. Lastly, what has His favor looked like in your life?

I encourage you to answer those questions and start thanking God like King David.

DAY 24

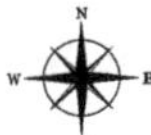

SUPERABUNDANTLY BLESSED

Isn't it amazing to imagine you're a superhero, a vigilante, or have a specific power? Envision you can fly, teleport, fight with unmatched strength, or run and swim quicker than lightning. This isn't just a figment of your imagination—*you are* a superhero—a real one—because the One Who lives within us is a superhero! Just read the following passage.

"Now to Him who is able to [carry out His purpose and] do superabundantly more than all that we dare ask or think [infinitely beyond our greatest prayers, hopes, or dreams], according to His power that is at work within us."

—EPHESIANS 3:20 (AMP)

"Much more will those who receive the abundance of grace and the free gift of righteousness reign in life through the one man Jesus Christ."

—ROMANS 5:17 (ESV)

Lord, I don't know what to write, but thank you, Jesus, for your extraordinary favor. Now, I understand who I am in Christ. I am loved, favored, forgiven, a child of God, blessed like a royal, a chosen prince, holy, free, and special. Lord, the benefits I have in You overwhelm me. Through Your Word and John Bevere's *Extraordinary,* I now know that:

1. I am made to reign and rule in this life.
2. I am made to rise above the norm.
3. I am an influencer now, not a follower.
4. I am a leader in my field.
5. I have been given a goldy life of the overcomer.
6. I am advanced in all areas of society.
7. I can be one of the most creative, innovative, winsome, and wisest people on earth.
8. I can overcome the world's powers and influence through your revelation of who I am.
9. I will not be defeated, condemned, and fruitless.

10. I will bear much fruit and be an imitator of God as his dear child.
11. As rulers in life, we, meet people's needs by the exceedingly great power that's in us. This is the victory that overcomes the world. It's our faith that causes us to rule in this life.

You are not just a man-made fictional superhero, but you are appointed by God, who created everything to be one.

The author also added:

How amazing are these words? It's not just abundantly beyond what we can ask or think, but superabundantly far over and above! If that isn't enough, Paul goes on to say "Infinitely beyond our highest prayers, desires, thoughts, hopes, or dreams!" Stop and ponder all this for just a moment. Infinitely beyond is past our human comprehension; it's extraordinary!"[26] *(author emphasis added)*

Isn't that wonderful! You are not just a man-made fictional superhero, but you are appointed by God, who created everything to be one.

DAY 25

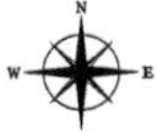

YOU ARE ROYALTY

Other people may think of you as inadequate or lacking, but always view yourself through the lens of the Bible. You are one of a kind, royal, holy, chosen, loved by God, and the apple of His eye.

"But you are a chosen generation, a royal priesthood, a holy nation, His own special people, that you may proclaim the praises of Him who called you out of darkness into His marvelous light."
–1 PETER 2:9

As I write, tears flow down my face. I marvel at the immensity of God's love and beautiful promises to me. I am just a mere sinner susceptible to mistakes; now, I am greatly showered by His love and favor and blessed with His God's goodness; I am complete, declared righteous through Jesus Christ with all the fullness of God and grace for grace I have seen and received.

Start walking in your identity in this dark world because it fulfills your purpose, shines a light into the lives of others, and pleases the One who created you.

Charles Stanley calls it "a flurry of wonderful descriptions to portray the exalted position we enjoy as believers in Christ." He says, "God calls us 'chosen' and 'royal' and 'holy' and 'special' so that we might begin to act like who we really are."[27]

Start walking in your identity in this dark world because it fulfills your purpose, shines a light into the lives of others, and pleases the One who created you.

DAY 26

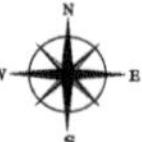

ONLY A LITTLE LOWER THAN GOD

Did you know that He created you a little lower than Himself? That means that we can perform the miracles Jesus performed, too. All we need is faith. God has given us His supernatural abilities and authority.

"Yet you made them only a little lower than God and crowned them with glory and honor. You gave them charge of everything you made, putting all things under their authority."
—PSALM 8:5–6 (NLT)

"I came so they can have real and eternal life, more and better life than they ever dreamed of."
—JOHN 10:10 (MSG)

Lord, thank you for these verses that empower me and encourage me to walk in my identity. I am excited about the extraordinary life You've given me. You tell me to live how You intended me to live—an extraordinary life that is not based on my job and what I do but on what You can do. It's about the disposition of my heart to live based on who I am in Christ. He has given us all authority over everything and in all things. I will use that authority to speak and claim God's promises. I will pray my prayers, dream my dreams, and ask for my desires as if I have already received them by faith! In Jesus' name!

By faith, speak life, healing, blessing, and favor over yourself and others like you have already received them!

In the same way, pray for what you want to happen in your life or the lives of others. By faith, speak life, healing, blessing, and favor over yourself and others like you have already received them!

DAY 27

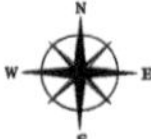

HE ACCOMPLISHES ALL

Wherever you are and whatever situation you are in, the Holy Spirit can creatively reveal things to you. Always expect the unexpected. Be open and ready to listen to His voice.

"You have granted me life and favor, And Your care has preserved my spirit."
—JOB 10:12

First, I just want to thank God for an excellent travel day yesterday. He protected me. At the airport, I prayed and claimed His promise in Jeremiah 33:3, "Call to Me, and I will answer you, and show you great and mighty things, which you do not know."

I am sitting on the airplane listening to God, and He impressed upon me that I am already living an extraordinary life of divine favor because He freely gave it to me. Thank you, Jesus!

He is like a compassionate friend, a great High Priest who can sympathize with all our troubles.

I see His goodness as I look back on the past few years.

2013

» I got my associate degree.

» He gave me three early promotion evaluations—the top out of three hundred other sailors in my rank.

» He allowed me to be a financial counselor, advising sailors under my command. Thank you, Lord. I have met sailors from different walks of life. I praise You that

I could go to the Legacy Class, Financial Peace University, Million-Dollar Sailor, and Command Financial Specialist training. I learned a lot through these classes.

2015

» I can see without my glasses. You gave me the desire to apply for Lasik surgery, and He provided it through the military for free.

» God showered me with extraordinary life and favor on Christmas. I was able to play with my brother Leo. I give You glory for the honor You've granted me.

» I could go to Ruby Falls, Cheesecake Factory, Rock Mountain, and the Tennessee state fair. I had a blast on my thirtieth birthday.

2016

» You promoted me to the next highest rank at the right time and place.

"He has made everything beautiful in its time."
—ECCLESIASTES 3:11

» As I checked in to USS Ford, I became known in the air department and the whole ship. They posted my picture and the other sailor on the ship for a piece about Asian American heritage. Everyone has told me that I am a famous superstar. Lord, I gave You all the credit. It's Your grace that makes it possible.

» I praise you, Jesus, for the extraordinary favor You showed me when my promotion picture with Kuya Leo went viral on Facebook.

» Thank you, Jesus. You awarded me the Navy achievement medal in front of the whole air department. I give You all the glory.

Whatever feeling you have and whatever situation you are in, I want you to come before the Holy Spirit. Tell Him to speak to you. Ask Him what He wants to say. He is like a compassionate friend, a great High Priest who can sympathize with all our troubles.

DAY 28

HE IS FAITHFUL AND TRUE

Have you ever felt like you were being falsely accused, judged, or unfairly criticized? Maybe out of nowhere, you felt like you were in the spotlight. Don't worry—the Holy Spirit will put words in your mouth and tell you what to say.

"The helpless commits himself to You; You are the helper of the fatherless."

—PSALM 10:14

"These things says the Amen, the Faithful and True Witness, the Beginning of the creation of God: 'I know your works, that you are neither cold nor hot. I could wish you were cold or hot.'"

—REVELATION 3:14

I went back to San Diego to visit my dad, and after that, I ate dinner with my Auntie and her daughter . It was very nice to see them, and I enjoyed being with them. I felt so welcomed and loved. The only problem is that my auntie asked me why my brothers and I acted the way we did about Dad, being uncaring and disrespectful to my Dad. Then, as I told them about our life as kids until now, I realized the hand of God had been intervening. God has showered me and my brothers with His extraordinary favor, love, protection, goodness, care, grace, mercy, blessing, and more. I call my Almighty God "Faithful and True." When I am unaware of my surroundings and feel helpless, God is with me to help, comfort, and strengthen me.

Finally, my Auntie understood our story and did not blame us. I praise you, Jesus!

Refrain from retaliating or reacting quickly out of emotion.

My most precious memory of an extraordinary life happened somewhere in-between December 14 and 16, 2016, when I took a vacation alone in San Diego. He really communicated with me as I spent time alone with Him. He also blessed me with a Camaro 2017 rental for five days. San Diego, California, is just as beautiful and lovely as it was four years ago.

The next time you feel like you are being falsely accused of something, like I felt when my Auntie called me and my brothers uncaring and disrespectful, just relax. Refrain from retaliating or reacting quickly out of emotion. Ask the Holy Spirit what to say and do. God will back you up.

DAY 29

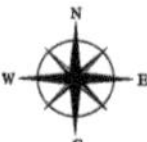

THE KING OF OUR HEARTS

Do you have stories of humble beginnings that grew into a much better lifestyle later? Aren't you amazed at how God moved and blessed you? Like Job, the Lord blessed his latter days more than his beginning (See Job 42:12).

"Oh, give thanks to the LORD, for He is good! For His mercy endures forever."
—PSALM 136:1

"For the LORD is good; His mercy is everlasting, And
His truth endures to all generations.
—PSALM 100:5

God is speaking of His goodness today. He is putting Sarah McMillan's song "King of My Heart" on my heart for worship.

I am asking God what to write, and He is telling me that He supplies all my needs—as in all—and gives me the desires of my heart. I remember when I needed money to get a ride to school but my aunt's friend took me instead. God blessed me mightily. Thank you, Jesus! I don't need to wait or ask someone to give me money. God has already showered me with abundant food, my own ride, and a hefty savings; He paid for my college tuition, clothing, rent, stable income, retirement, investments, and more.

God also blessed me with a free keyboard, guitar, and banjo to top it all off. Thank you, Father. I praise God that I was able to drive a Camaro. That wouldn't have been an option in the Philippines.

In reality, it is because of God's mercy and compassion that we experience abundance or even just the little blessings of life, like waking up every morning.

I saw a young guy on the internet who had just been released from jail in 2016. A lot of ladies liked his mug shot. He posted on Facebook about his new house, car, and family. Then I realized God had impressed on me that I could have used all those years—a life wasted in jail, probably three or four years—to serve God at a local church, minister, or do something productive. I would not trade my experiences in God's presence and the places God has taken me, such as Thailand, Singapore, Australia, and the Philippines (Cebu), for anything! Thank you, Father. I would not trade my brothers and sisters in Christ for anything, either. Most importantly, I would never sell God's extraordinary favor, blessing, approval, joy, peace, grace, and power, nor forfeit an intimate relationship with Him!

In reality, it is because of God's mercy and compassion that we experience abundance or even just the little blessings of life, like waking up every morning.

DAY 30

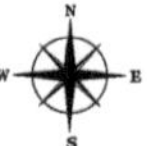

IT IS WELL

It is calming when a friend, brother, or sister assures you that everything will be okay during your darkest hour! The Bible reminds us that Jesus Christ says the same thing because He is sympathetic and compassionate.

Seeing then that we have a great High Priest who has passed through the heavens, Jesus the Son of God, let us hold fast our confession. For we do not have a High Priest who cannot sympathize with our weaknesses, but was in all points tempted as we are, yet without sin. Let us therefore come boldly to the throne of grace, that we may obtain mercy and find grace to help in time of need.

—HEBREWS 4:14–16

God told me three things last Sunday: "Everything is going to be alright! Everything is going to be fine and excellent! Everything is going to be well!" Thank you, Father! These apply to all aspects of my life. Hillsong's "It is Well with My Soul" also came to mind.

Listen to Jesus Christ's soft voice telling you that everything will be fine!

During our Sunday service, Pastor Larry made a lasting impression on my spirit. He said, "Our circumstances never define us because our circumstances are not who we are. We are always made in God's image."

I don't know where you came from or what circumstances you are in, but I want to encourage you to listen to Jesus Christ's soft voice telling you that everything will be fine!

DAY 31

FAITH

Fear influences our decisions. Whether minor or significant, we must base our decisions on what God wants us to do instead of our feelings. I encourage you to prioritize obedience and intimacy with God. It is the way to wisdom and favor.

"I can do all things through Christ who strengthens me."

—PHILIPPIANS 4:13

"Jesus said to him, 'If you can believe, all things are possible to him who believes.'"

—MARK 9:23

Thank you, Father, for You have done great and mighty things in my life yet again! You have given me excellent experiences and revealed Your power in my life.

I almost didn't play the keyboard during Sunday's worship service last week because one of the songs was too hard. I wasn't sure what would happen if I declined the invitation to play. Then God told me to have faith in Him, trust Him, obey Him, and leave all the consequences to Him.

I asked my brother, Leo, if I was playing that week. He advised me not to back out just because of one song. So, I went to rehearsal. Everyone greeted me. I also prayed for the first time in our group devotion. Thank you, Father, for the confidence You gave me. It got better—our worship leader, Shawn, asked me to play for communion! That was a sign of God's favor and approval. Lord, I can't deny Your extraordinary favor on my life.

I talked a bit with Mike Henry, our church saxophone player, and felt well-rested that Wednesday because I was off work. I was supposed to stand watch at work on Friday and Sunday nights, but they secured the watches. So, I was able to attend my community group. We fellowshipped. I was very encouraged and felt love for my brothers and sisters in Christ. Michael, our community group leader, also let me lead and say an opening prayer for my community group. I tasted and saw God's extraordinary love.

My agreement to play the keyboard last Sunday was an act of obedience, and because of it, He showered me with extraordinary favor and blessing. His presence, love, grace, healing, anointing, and power were manifested in the service. Glory to you, Jesus! I give You the highest praise and honor, God. You are worthy.

After the service, John and Melissa winked at me as a sign of approval. Thank you for them, Jesus. Shawn, Mike Henry, Seth, and Mrs. Jane said, "Sounds good," and "Good job, Andrew." Jesus, I give you, all the compliments, adoration, talent, and gifts.

Whether you are a new or mature Christian, your obedience to Him separates you from others because His blessing will permeate every aspect of your life.

This event reminds me of "Nativity," the theme of our church event during Christmas back in December 2015, which reminds me of the extraordinary life, favor, love, grace, and blessing He has given me. God also gave me a song titled "Nothing is Impossible" by Planetshakers. Be encouraged as you listen to it.

Whether you are a new or mature Christian, your obedience to Him separates you from others because His blessing will permeate every aspect of your life. It is a way of living a life at its very best. You'll be glad you did it.

DAY 32

YOU'RE A CHILD OF GOD

Do you realize the benefit of being a child of a God? Not a child of a president, celebrity, or great athlete, but of God Himself, Jesus Christ—His innate qualities and completeness manifested in you. As heirs, everything that belongs to God (which is everything) also belongs to you.

"Surely goodness and mercy shall follow me All the days of my life; And I will dwell in the house of the LORD forever."

—PSALM 23:6

"The Spirit Himself bears witness with our spirit that we are children of God, and if children, then heirs—heirs of God and joint heirs with Christ, if indeed we suffer with Him, that we may also be glorified together."

—ROMANS 8:16

God gave me these two verses on March 5th while I was at church. A sense of peace and calmness embraced me as I claimed His promise of peace in Philippians 4:4-7 the night before.

Rejoice in the Lord always. Again I will say, rejoice! Let your gentleness be known to all men. The Lord is at hand. Be anxious for nothing, but in everything by prayer and supplication with thanksgiving, let your requests be made known to God; and the peace of God, which surpasses all understanding, will guard your hearts and minds through Christ Jesus.

I went home and asked God what He was trying to say in these two verses and whether I should write them down. As I listened to Him, He gave me a song by Jonathan and Melissa Helser, "No Longer Slaves." God reminded me of Romans 8:15 through that song: "For you did not receive the spirit of bondage again to fear, but you received the Spirit of adoption by whom we cry out, 'Abba, Father.'" The MSG translation says it this way: "God's Spirit beckons. There are things to do and places to go! This resurrection life you received from God is not a timid, grave-tending life. It's adventurously expectant, greeting God with a childlike 'What's next, Papa?'"

God whispered to me, "Don't be afraid of the Plan Maintenance System, your leadership at work, or SKED 3.2 (the software we use for the Plan Maintenance System).

"For God has not given us a spirit of fear, but a spirit of power and of love and of a sound mind."
–2 Timothy 1:7

Your life in Christ as a child of God is adventurous, exciting, and expectant. It is extraordinary.

I am no longer a slave to fear but a child of God. He will help me; He will be with me wherever I go. Goodness and mercy will follow me all the days of my life (at work, home, church, school, and everywhere else). I will enjoy this command. It will be exciting because I will travel to lovely places and experience God's extraordinary favor and help.

Your life in Christ as a child of God is adventurous, exciting, and expectant. It is extraordinary.

DAY 33

DREAMS

Did you know that God Himself can make our dreams and desires come true more than we can? When you surrender your life to Him and continually obey Him, you will see a glimpse of fulfilled dreams coming true without even realizing it.

I have to share what God revealed to me. First, He led me to Psalms 103. Then I ask God what He wanted to say through that verse. Later, I had a dream about my life and how I used to be—in bondage, gripped by lust. Then God reminded me how He freed, forgave, blessed, healed, and crowned me with favor and loving-kindness. A once hopeless life toward destruction is now redeemed, destined for health, prosperity, an extraordinary life, and favor.

"For I know the plans I have for you," says the Lord, "plans for well-being and not for trouble, to give you a future and a hope."

—JEREMIAH 29:11 (NLV)

"Praise the Lord, O my soul. And forget none of His acts of kindness. He forgives all my sins. He heals all my diseases. He saves my life from the grave. He crowns me with loving-kindness and pity. He fills my years with good things and I am made young again like the eagle."

—PSALM 103: 2–5 (NLV)

Second, God revealed His sovereignty. He gave me John 10:10, and I explored it different translations.

"I came so they might have life, a great full life" (NLV).

"My purpose is to give life in all its fullness" (TLB).

"My purpose is to give them a rich and satisfying life" (NLT).

"I have come that they may have life and that they may have it more abundantly."

Trust His process of making your dreams and desires come true.

These have impacted my life. What the devil means to destroy, God uses to bless and give the abundant life full of healing and all good things! Watching *Ben-Hur*, I was awakened to God's goodness. I praise Him for what He has done for our family! Because of His love, my brothers and I were able to come to America with our father.

Now, I can see my dad and live in America, a country full of opportunities and prosperity.

Trust His process of making your dreams and desires come true. Continually surrender your life to Him and obey Him. You'll be amazed!

DAY 34

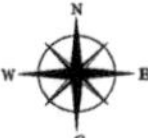

SUPER DAD

God puts your family in your life as an encouragement, a source of wisdom, love, comfort, help, and a safe haven. Your family is no accident. Knowingly or unknowingly, they have shaped you into who you are.

"I know what I'm doing, I have it all planned out—plans to take care of you, not to abandon you, plans to give you the future you hope for."
—JEREMIAH 29:11 (MSG)

"For I know the plans I have for you," says the Lord, "plans for well-being and not for trouble, to give you future and a hope."
—JEREMIAH 29:11 (NLV)

God blesses us with these verses. Although my dad is in the hospital, God has a plan for him—to bring healing, blessing, prosperity, extraordinary favor, and an expected end. I was going out for a walk on the beach when my brother called and shared a quote from Maury Davis's devotional *The Last Ride*: "Your life can be richer than your heritage if you create the power of favor in it. You can exceed your birthright with the gift of favor."[28]

Pray for them, visit them, and embrace them.

Is there someone in your family who gives you comfort and wisdom? Who is your safe haven? Pray for them, visit them, and embrace them. Most importantly, thank God for bringing them into your life.

DAY 35

THE GOD WHO ACTS

Do you feel you've waited long enough for something you've prayed about? The Bible is full of wonderful promises to those who wait for Him.

"For since the beginning of the world Men have not heard nor perceived by the ear, Nor has the eye seen any God besides You, who acts for the one who waits for Him."

—ISAIAH 64:4

The Holy Spirit is speaking to me even as I write. I experience God's best because I wait for Him. He gave me some examples.

During my helpless month of fixing and healing my anger toward my dad, God intervened by sending me to boot camp and other schools to mold me. Finally, when the time was right, I enjoyed fellowship with my dad, and my anger disappeared.

Next, I've waited for God's direction before entering into a relationship. When He presented a lady in 2018, it was the most enjoyable and satisfying dating experience I have ever had. In my learning, I am glorifying Him. Thank you, Jesus. Being in love is such a unique experience!

My time with my mom in the Philippines was an incredible experience. Her love nourished me as a kid. Every event in my life as a child was planned and God-ordained. If I am being honest, life in the Philippines without my mom after she passed away was challenging. Her source of love and help was gone because of her passing. Yet God intervened. Even in those times, God's hand was upon me. After four years of waiting, I finished high school after my mom passed. We flew to America, and my life has never been the same again. God likes to bless me and my brothers with delicious food we've never tried. We've visited new places and met different people.

Thank you, Jesus! God allowed me to travel worldwide and visit different countries in the US Navy. Not only that, but I thank Him for sending me to another school while in the Navy. The school was fun and exciting to study.

When I hit my ten-year mark in the Navy and made first class petty officer, I felt like everything went by slowly. I was dragging in the Navy. As I waited on the Lord, He blessed me mightily and opened up new opportunities to show me His favor. Thank you, Jesus! While on a US Ship named Gerald R. Ford, I became a leading petty officer and work center supervisor. There, I honed my leadership skills and became the mess deck master at arm.

The waiting season of your life is always well-spent.

After my term in the US Ship Gerald R. Ford, I picked two of the best schools as an electrician's mate: The Electrician's Mate Surface Ship Electrical Advance Maintenance and Landing Helicopter Dock-1 Electrical Component Maintenance Technician Pipeline. I love you, Jesus, for sending me to these schools. I'm grateful for letting me stay in a friendly, fully paid hotel worth $20,000. While there, I tried delicious food like pancakes, pizza, and chicken wings. I also praise God for introducing me to Mrs. Julie and her family. Her family and the church made me feel welcomed.

The Lord is full of surprises—far more than you could think or ask—as you wait. You are favored and loved by God. He is well aware of every detail of your life. The waiting season of your life is always well-spent.

DAY 36

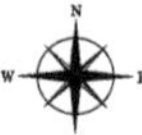

BLESSED ARE ALL THOSE WHO WAIT FOR HIM

Whether you like it or not, waiting on the Lord produces favorable results. When have you experienced the frustration of waiting? The fruitfulness? If you have ever waited on the Lord, you have or will see His great plan in your life unfold. Be expectant and rejoice!

"But this is what I commanded them, saying, 'Obey my voice, and I will be your God, and you shall be My people. And walk in all the ways that I have commanded you, that it may be well with you.'"
—JEREMIAH 7:23

Sister Ellen told me to read the whole chapter of Jeremiah 7, but verse 23 captured my eyes. According to Charles Stanley, *God desires prosperity for you. He wants you to be a whole person, balanced and growing and fruitful and fulfilling His purpose for your life. So ask yourself: What do I desire? How am I acting on it?*[29]

He continues to open the door to new opportunities as I share my stories about waiting on the Lord. While I was in a Ticonderoga-class cruiser ship waiting for deployment to be over, God blessed me with many new and exciting experiences:

- » I got to ride in a helicopter.
- » Also, before deployment started, I stayed in a beachside hotel for three to four days. I have always wanted to stay on the oceanfront in Virginia Beach, Virginia. Thank you, Jesus.
- » My favorite salad back in the United States is Greek salad. I always wondered how Greek salads taste in Greece. Guess what? This deployment stopped in Greece and Bahrain, and I got to try it!
- » During deployment, I experienced working out and running along the beach because the gym on the ship was outside. It was such a nice view!
- » Each and every day, God surprises me as I wait. I have learned about engineering plants and have saved substantial money.

- If I were home, I would be unable to watch the National Basketball Association during playoffs. Here, we have all the NBA channels.
- Also, my leadership skills are improving. I have a lot of time to read books and enjoy the mentorship of other leaders. Thank you, Jesus.
- Lastly, the favor of God is showering upon me. I get to play my keyboard with my band of brothers. I would not have Kuya Leo's keyboard if I had not been deployed. I think this message in Jeremiah 7:23 emphasizes that God wants me to obey His voice so that I may experience a whole and complete life, and right now, I am experiencing it. I love you, Jesus!

Charles Stanley says, "God desires for you to be a whole person, growing in the likeness of Jesus Christ, fruitful and fulfilling His purpose for your life. He also assumes full responsibility for your needs when you obey Him."[30]

Lord, You are unique, a very creative and loving God!

Therefore, the LORD will wait, that He may be gracious to you; And therefore He will be exalted, that He may have mercy on you. For the LORD is a God of justice; Blessed are all those who wait for Him.
—ISAIAH 30:18

God's surprises and blessings above measure made me want to finish strong in the Navy as I waited to complete my twenty-plus years of service. Though I am single right now, I get to experience so many wonderful things (like eating lobster every month!). I am at my prime, experiencing the best of everything. Not all people have the opportunity to live near the ocean. Lord, You are unique, a very creative and loving God!

Charles Stanley once said:

The Lord wants the very best for us. At times, this includes delaying His response until the perfect time arrives. Is the Lord tarrying in some important situation in your life? Have you been waiting a long time for some precious promise? Remember, God works on behalf of those who wait for Him. He has not forgotten you; He is moving behind the scenes for your benefit. Be patient and trust Him because the One who longs to be gracious to you is waiting until the blessing He has for you is perfected.[31]

Ask God to show you all the good things He has done for you during your waiting season. Write down what you learned and the exciting things you've experienced. You will be amazed at how God works in your life, pouring out His favor and love on you.

DAY 37

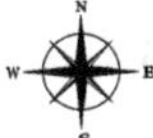

LIVE LIKE THIS

The Bible is full of practical advice. It is easy to understand and accessible to the public. It is neither rocket science nor a secret formula that only a few can know. God is more than willing to reveal His plan for your life.

"And now, Israel, what does the LORD your God require of you, but to fear the LORD your God, to walk in all His ways and to love Him, to serve the LORD your God with all your heart and with all your soul."

—DEUTERONOMY 10:12

I am excited to share the word I received from God today. I asked Him some questions about serving in the church here on board the ship USS Monterey and He gave me this verse. According to Charles Stanley,

> *God commanded the Israelites to take Canaan; but after 40 years of wandering, no doubt they wondered if they had what it took to wage a successful campaign. Yet, God did not expect them to have a perfect battle plan. Rather, He simply wanted them to love and obey Him. Moses understood that Israel couldn't be under God's protection without obedience and faith, so he reminded them of the essence of God's law: (1) fear God; (2) walk in His ways; (3) love Him; (4) serve Him wholeheartedly; and (5) obey Him. God isn't an impossible taskmaster, He won't set you up to fail. Rather, He is your loving God who is making a way for you through whatever challenges you face. Your responsibility is to walk in His ways.*[32]

God doesn't expect me to have a perfect plan. Instead, He wants me to just love and obey Him.

With five years left in the Navy before I am eligible to retire like the Israelites, God doesn't expect me to have a perfect plan. Instead, He wants me to just love and obey Him. To enjoy His presence and the benefits of it. Who knows, maybe He wants me to stay more than or less than five years.

So, God's response to my question was that it's not a matter of whether I am busy or shy in playing my keyboard; it's just about serving Him who is the Lord, my God, with all my heart, according to Deuteronomy 10:12. God promises to bless all those who live like this.

You are in good hands for the rest of your life here on this earth when you fear God, walk in His ways, love Him, serve Him wholeheartedly, and obey Him. You can't go wrong with that. People who live like this experience life at its very best.

DAY 38

SATISFACTION OR REGRET

Have you seen successful billionaires in their field whose health is deteriorating? So you know of someone famous or talented who received great recognition from others yet didn't know or serve Jesus Christ? Would you really want to trade places with them?

"Unless the LORD builds the house, they labor in vain who build it; Unless the LORD guards the city, the watchman stays awake in vain."

—PSALM 127:1

Thank you, God, for Psalm 127:1. Like my cousin, many people might feel proud and accomplished for making it to the other side, but it's useless if they don't know the Lord or accept Him as their personal Savior.

Most importantly, always partner with Him to do what He wants.

According to Charles Stanley, "All our efforts are useless and futile if we do not partner with God in what He wants, and in the time and manner He desires to accomplish it. The blessing of the Lord spells the difference between success and failure, satisfaction and regret."[33]

Do you feel content and happy with your life because you know the Lord? Has He given you divine health and wealth of spirit? If you have the Lord Jesus Christ, you have everything. Thank God for everything He has given you on this earth that you enjoy! Most importantly, always partner with Him to do what He wants.

DAY 39

PEACE IN SINGLEHOOD

Are you currently single or married? What are some of the greatest lessons or gifts you've received during those seasons of your life? Whatever your status, God has tremendous benefits and promises for those who delight in His word, those who trust and hope in Him, and those who don't walk in the counsel of the ungodly.

The Holy Spirit gave me three Scriptures while on deployment. I asked Him what He wanted to say to me through them, and He gave me a fresh revelation of their benefits. First is Psalms 1:1-3:

Blessed is the man
Who walks not in the counsel of the ungodly,
Nor stands in the path of sinners;
Nor sits in the seat of the scornful;
But his delight is in the law of the Lord,
And in His law he meditates day and night.
He shall be like a tree
Planted by the rivers of water,
That brings forth its fruits in its season,
Whose leaf also shall not wither;
And whatever he does shall prosper.

Today, I am thankful I've returned from deployment. I am still trying to decide whether to even write a story. I'm not even quite sure what I intend to tell!

God then gave me Psalm 92:12–14. "The righteous shall flourish like a palm tree, He shall grow like a cedar in Lebanon. Those who are planted in the house of the LORD shall flourish in the courts of our God. They shall still bear fruit in old age; They shall be fresh and flourishing."

If you are still single and unmarried, don't become impatient, because you are blessed either way.

Jeremiah 17:7-8 was the last one:

Blessed is the man who trusts in the LORD, and whose hope is the LORD. For he shall be like a tree planted by the waters, Which spreads out its roots by the river, And will not fear when heat comes; But its leaf will be green, And will not be anxious in the year of drought, Nor will cease from yielding fruit.

Now, let's break it down. Meditate on each segment and ask the Lord for your own revelation.

PSALM 1:3

1. Whatever he does shall prosper.
2. Whose leaf also shall not wither.
3. That brings forth its fruit in its season.

PSALM 92: 12-14

1. The righteous shall flourish like a palm tree.
2. He shall grow like a cedar in Lebanon. Woodland trust defines a cedar as "a majestic, evergreen conifer which can grow to 35m/98 to 115 feet."[34]
3. They shall still bear fruit in old age (longevity).
4. They shall be fresh and flourishing.

JEREMIAH 17:7-8

1. Blessed is the man who trusts in the Lord.
2. Will not fear when the heat comes.
3. And will not be anxious in the year of drought.
4. Will not cease from yielding fruit.
5. Which spreads out its roots by the river.
6. But its leaf will be green.

Today, these verses encouraged me the most in the area of my singlehood. Wow! What a fantastic promise of God for you. If you are still single and unmarried, don't become impatient, because you are blessed either way.

DAY 40

TRUST AND OBEDIENCE

Have you ever asked yourself if you made the right or wrong choice about some significant decision in your life? I have great news: once you accept and believe that Jesus Christ is your Savior, the Holy Spirit is living within you to guide and comfort you in whatever you're facing, including the tough decisions you have to make.

I am thankful for a refreshing and restful vacation. I saw my niece and their dogs, Keejay and Daisy. I praise God for the delicious food. My ex-girlfriend texted me and invited me to have coffee with her, but God instructed me to move on. So, I obeyed! After I went home, I felt a little regret and asked God if I had done the right thing. I wasn't confident whether this instruction was from God or not. I felt a little sad. I scanned social media and found a post by Dr. Caroline Leaf:

> *Sometimes, the right decisions feel so wrong and hurt so much. So how do you know if it was, or is, the right decision? That comes down to a combination of seeing and understanding yourself through self-regulation and self-awareness, receiving advice and counsel from trusted people like a therapist, and, of course, hope and faith.*
>
> *It's never easy and it may take time to feel good about your decision, but I promise you will get there. Give yourself time to mourn and feel your feelings. Suppressing and ignoring won't help—it will only make things worse!*[35]

I need God's grace more than ever. Following Dr. Leaf's wisdom, I'm relieved that it is normal to grieve over the right decisions.

I drove around to look for houses and found a safe, lovely home by the beach. God gave me the verse in Genesis 24:1, "Now Abraham was old, well advanced in age; and the LORD blessed Abraham in all things."

I can count on God's blessings because I obeyed Him—I did not give into temptation and see my ex-girlfriend. His verse felt like confirmation that He will give me a fully paid house by the beach, in a safe neighborhood, and that I will profit from it. It is the kind of house that I really, really like and will enjoy.

While I was talking to my brother, Dexter, he prophesied Ephesians 3:20 over me, "Now to Him who is able to do exceedingly abundantly above all that we ask or think, according to the power that works in us, to Him be glory in the church of Christ Jesus to all generations forever and ever."

When God said these things, He wasn't just referring to the house, but physically, spiritually, emotionally, financially, as a steward of my talents both in church and in the Navy, and in all other relationships. According to Charles Stanley, "Would you like to be blessed 'in all things,' as Abraham was? Then you must follow Abraham's example of trust and obedience, for that is the way to great blessing."[36]

Spend some time listening to Him.

Ask God for direction the next time you need counsel or advice. The Holy Spirit will speak as vividly and clearly to you as He did to me. He uses God's Word, other people, dreams, vision, and sometimes His still, small voice. Spend some time listening to Him. Trust me, you will have confidence in your decision at the end of the day.

DAY 41

THE GOD WHO FIGHTS FOR YOU

"No man shall be able to stand before you all the days of your life; as I was with Moses, so I will be with you. I will not leave you nor forsake you."

—JOSHUA 1:5

First of all, I thank God for giving me promises today. I can't help but write about it. I went to my community group last Monday, and we were asked the question, "When was a time you faced difficulties but persevered, and things eventually turned around for the better?" I didn't say anything but asked myself and God the same question as I drove home. Finally, God spoke and reminded me of my experience when I first arrived in Virginia in 2013. I didn't know anyone at first besides my brother, Leo. I saved $40,000 but have a $85,000 mortgage for a house that my other brother, Dexter, cosigned. On my way to Virginia, the Navy sent me to my first Navy enlisted classification school, but I failed and dropped the class. I was so disappointed! Yet God was on the move!

It's almost eight years since that happened, and God has turned it around. He showed me the great and mighty things He has done for me, and all I could do was cry and worship Him.

1. He let me save $245,000 for a newer, fully paid car.
2. I am now living in an apartment with privacy.
3. He let me attend and finish four Navy enlisted classification schools. I also got my associate degree.
4. I fully paid my mortgage and got out of the cosign. Now, I am about to buy my own house.
5. God gave me a local church where I could serve and fellowship. Thank you, Jesus!
6. He promoted me to first class petty officer in the Navy, the rank which will allow me to retire. Plus, by faith, I have another promotion coming.
7. He blesses me with beautiful relationships with friends and family. Thank you, Father.

8. I praise You, God, for deploying me on the East Coast so that I could visit Israel. I am grateful that You granted me the desire of my heart.

"Delight yourself also in the LORD, and He shall give you the desires of your heart."

—PSALM 37:4

According to Charles Stanley, "When we make the Lord our joy, the desires that grow in our hearts are usually the ones He plants. These are the things that bring lasting peace and satisfaction—not the things we think we want or strive to achieve apart from God."[37]

He will move in your life in a mighty way.

I told Sister Ellen that God gave me Joshua 1:4 and Genesis 24:1. She told me these verses are conditional promises if I obey God wholeheartedly.

"Now Abraham was old, well advanced in age; and the LORD had blessed Abraham in all things."

—GENESIS 24:1

"From the wilderness and this Lebanon as far as the great river, the River Euphrates, all the land of the Hittites, and to the Great Sea toward the going down of the sun, shall be your territory."

—JOSHUA 1:4

Stanley asked, "Would you like to be blessed "in all things" as Abraham was? Then you must follow Abraham's example of trust and obedience, for that is the way to great blessing."[38]

Doesn't knowing that God is fighting for you excite and amaze you? I pray that God makes you wholeheartedly obedient, loyal, and faithful to Him in everything. He will move in your life in a mighty way. I encourage you to listen to "Egypt" by Cory Asbury.

"When we do God's will in God's way with God's help, no one and nothing can stand in the way of our success. The key is the presence of the Lord."[39]

—CHARLES STANLEY

DAY 42

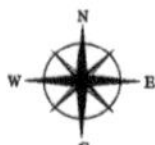

SUPERNATURAL LIVING

Have you ever felt content and happy after God delivered you out of difficult situations or trials? It's like gratefulness and joy engulfs your life. After a while, you look back and realize that, despite adversities, God's hand was on your life, supplying all your needs, and protecting and blessing you.

After nine months of deployment (thank You, Jesus), I am home now, drinking milk tea. Lord, I realized You've supplied all my needs throughout my deployment. Even though we're in the middle of the ocean, I have unlimited supplies of wipes, herbal tea, books, sleep, and other necessities. I returned home with a fully furnished apartment and a car ready for me. Hallelujah!

God has put Proverbs 3:5-6 on my heart today: "Trust in the Lord with all your heart, And lean not on your own understanding; In all your ways acknowledge Him, and He shall direct your paths."

In his book, Stanley observes:

If you want your life to be the very best it can be, you must put your full faith in God, reject your own limited perspective, and honor Him in every area of your life. This is the heart of godly living–you submit to the Lord's direction, knowing that He has the answer to your every need and is faithful to provide (Philippians 4:19).[40]

When you experience resistance and hardship, view it as an opportunity to become spiritually mature in Christ, get increased favor and grace, receive a new level of authority, and lavish in the chance to glorify God.

I started worshiping, crying, and thanking God as He showed me His lavishing generosity towards me. I love you, Jesus! Sister Ellen said that I am now experiencing supernatural living. I expect beautiful things to happen in my life. Hallelujah!

When you experience resistance and hardship, view it as an opportunity to become spiritually mature in Christ, get increased favor and grace, receive a new level of authority, and lavish in the chance to glorify God.

DAY 43

FALLING TO GRACE

Did you know that even if you make mistakes or sin, God can weave them into something beautiful? They are His hidden gems, and blessings can flow out of them. This is only possible because of the GRACE of God.

"If you diligently heed the voice of the LORD your God and do what is right in His sight, give ear to His commandments and keep all His statutes, I will put none of the diseases on you which I have brought on the Egyptians. For I am the LORD who heals you."

—EXODUS 15:26

I stood watch at the Central Control Station on the ship and prayed and listened to God. For some reason, I suddenly felt the favor of God on every aspect of my life. As I submitted and offered up my dating life to God, I realized I feel the love of others now more than ever because I am getting closer and closer to Jesus. In addition, He gave me Deuteronomy 7:9. "Therefore, know that the Lord your God, He is God, the faithful God who keeps covenant and mercy for a thousand generations with those who love Him and keep His commandments."

Today, I gave in to temptation. While at church, God reminded me of all the times I fell into the temptation to remind me how He has loved and sustained me despite my sin:

» September to December 2007
» March and October 2013
» May 2019
» June-July 2020
» February 2022

God reminded me that He loved me even before my struggle with lust began. Nothing can separate me from the love of God. I was reading my journal entry from July 2, 2020. The entry was all about the great and mighty things He has done in my life, and how they far surpass the weight of my sin. I've experienced His love and grace more than the ache of my guilt—way, way more.

God asked me to count the many times He healed me.

1. Restoring my vision so that I could see without glasses.
2. Healing my ulcer.
3. Showing me that the source of my stomach pain was overeating. I was able to heal it because of this revelation.
4. Curing my ingrown toenail. Thank you, Jesus.
5. Healing me from possible COVID—and fast!
6. Fixing a crack in my tooth during deployment.

As Steven Furtick said, "Your greatest wisdom might come after your biggest mistake."[41] I understand what he was saying, but I would revise it to say: "Our greatest mistakes create our greatest experiences of His grace, comfort, blessing, and joy!" Hallelujah!

In fact, repentance turns God's wrath into favor.

I want to include the promises found in Matthew 5:4: "Blessed are those who mourn, for they shall be comforted." I realized that during those falls, when I cried, repented, and mourned about it, I experienced the comfort of God. It is evident in my life how often God intervenes as I trust and hope in Him. I love you, Jesus.

So the next time you fall short, stop feeling guilty. God's love for you is indescribable; it has no end. In fact, repentance turns God's wrath into favor.

DAY 44

REST

The Bible has several stories regarding God as a giver of rest to His people. In the same way, God can grant you rest, which includes peace and safety. When you obey Him and walk in all His ways, you can be assured of His rest in your life, just like in the story of King Jehoshaphat in 2 Chronicles 20:29.

"The Spirit Himself bears witness with our spirit that we are children of God, and if children, then heirs—heirs of God and joint heirs with Christ, if indeed we suffer with Him, that we may also glorified together."

—ROMANS 8:16

What joy I have today. I learned something new today after reviewing my journal entry from September 2021. After all of the bitter experiences from serving in the Navy, like the times my supervisor or chief yelled at me, the more challenging moments during my deployment, or when my crew gave me a hard time, I can now celebrate, because it's finally over! I reaped from the seeds I sowed during those trials. Right now, I have rest, peace, joy, and blessing, and I am safe.

One note I made in that entry says, "Everything that belongs to our Father belongs to us because we are heirs. Can you imagine that? The earth, ocean, and any human invention." As my realtor and I hunted for houses this weekend, I saw the ocean and felt this tremendous sense of peace knowing that everything God created and owned has also been given to me. Thank you, Jesus. Now that I have experienced those trials and know they are over, there is new wisdom and greater glory, authority, and power prevailing in me.

According to John Bevere,

"No matter the pressure of the thlipsis (tribulation) you encounter, the difficulty is nothing compared to the level of rulership you'll walk in after the tribulation has passed."[42]

Last Thursday, while on duty, God gave me a verse in James 1:2-4: "My brethren, count it all joy when you fall into various trials, knowing that the testing of your faith produces patience. But let patience have its perfect work, that you may be perfect and complete, lacking nothing."

The reward and blessing of rest you will receive after your temporary trials will far outweigh any pain you experience.

I finally get to check out of this arduous command and go to easy shore duty command. My supervisors, the senior chief, chief engineer, top snipes, and other leaders have trained me intensely. Praise God it's over!

God continues to remind me of what He has promised me, and He will do the same for you. The reward and blessing of rest you will receive after your temporary trials will far outweigh any pain you experience.

DAY 45

JUST TRUST AND BE FAITHFUL

Nowadays, multiple books have been written on how to achieve your dreams and desires. Some authors will even show you how to succeed based on their own experience, but I believe each of us has his or her unique way of succeeding. We have different dreams and desires that God planted in our hearts.

"Delight yourself also in the LORD, and He shall give you the desires of your heart."

—PSALM 37:4

"When you make the Lord your joy, the desires that grow in your heart are usually the ones He plants. These are the things that bring lasting peace and satisfaction—not the things we think we want or strive to achieve apart from God."

—CHARLES STANLEY

It's May 16, 2022. I'm not sure what to write, but I know that my heart is full of awe and gratitude. On June 3, 2020, I wrote, "His love and grace are greater." His favor overflows despite our sin or wrong thinking. He has given me opportunities to travel worldwide, save up, and finish school. He blessed me with a lady who loved me. In short, He lifts me to my feet and plants me on solid ground. I love you, Jesus.

"Surely goodness and mercy shall follow me All the days of my life; And I will dwell in the house of the LORD Forever."

—PSALM 23:6

It is sometimes hard to see God's goodness, especially when we have bad days. From now on, I'm committed to reading past journal entries and meditating on His faithfulness.

On July 17, 2020, I wrote, "I am loved." I've seen God answer prayers and fulfill dreams. I dreamed of seeing without my glasses again, so He healed me. I had dreams of visiting Disneyland, so He made it happen! I visited Disneyland, Universal Studios, Bush Gardens, and Great America, and I've had the privilege of living in the US. Wow! That's a full-package deal! Also, when I was a kid, I saw a plane fly by as I was playing outside. I prayed, "Lord, I want to ride a plane one day." What did He do? Answered it. Amazing! This is only one example of many.

One time, when I was at my brother's church, I noticed this young lady, Kelsey (my ex-girlfriend). She was pretty and young. I didn't ask God for her, but I got to know her intimately after two to three years. We went places I had never been to, and I met her family. God knows the desires of our hearts. He is good at keeping track of them even when we don't pray for them all.

His destiny for you is the best and most satisfying because He knows everything about you.

"Now to Him who is able to do exceedingly abundantly above all that we ask or think, according to the power that works in us."
—EPHESIANS 3:20

Just trust and be faithful. Many of the blessings in my life were not on my goal or prayer list. God just presented them. Thank you, Father. I give you all glory, honor, and praise.

In closing, whether you pursue your dreams and desires or read books on how to achieve them, God will fulfill them. His destiny for you is the best and most satisfying because He knows everything about you. John Bevere says, "His plans for you were set before you were formed in your mother's womb. No man, woman, or devil can ever get us out of the will of God! No one but God holds our destiny."[43]

DAY 46

BIKING AT THE BEACH

Do you love new things, like new relationships, places to visit, food, hobbies, or cars? Well, our heavenly Father loves new things, too. What He has done in your life before might be different from what He wants to do in your life right now. Always expect the unexpected.

Yesterday, I had one of the best experiences I have had in a while. I rode a bike by the beach for an hour and a half. Not only was I able to exercise, but I was also able to enjoy the view and listen to God. While riding a bike, God dropped Isaiah 43:19 on my heart: "Behold, I will do a new thing, Now it shall spring forth; Shall you not know it? I will even make a road in the wilderness And rivers in the desert."

I don't know what God wants to say here, but I know many new things are happening in my life. I got a new command (workplace) and a new place to live because I bought a house. Also, I am experiencing new things after reading books like *Intentional Living* by John Maxwell.

I am now pursuing things I am passionate about—violin, skateboarding, and basketball. I have also inquired about school because I am back on shore duty.

The Holy Spirit is leading me to read books that are changing me, like Stephen Covey's *Speed of Trust* and Michaell Hyatt's *No-Fail Communication*. They are transforming the way I lead at work. I like the change. Dr. Caroline Leaf's books have also given me new insight into health.

Robert Kiyosaki's *Rich Dad, Poor Dad* and Ryan Frederick's *Right Place, Right Time* have given me wisdom about buying a house and investing. Susie Moore's book *Stop Checking Your Likes* helped me to enjoy life more. Thank you, Jesus, for those books.

You will never be bored with God's plan and will in your life.

Lastly, I thank God for John Bevere's book *Relentless*. It has helped me to live and walk extraordinarily for Jesus. As His heirs, God uses trials to unlock our authority, wisdom, grace, favor, and power. Bevere's *The Bait of Satan* has also helped me with my long-time problem with control. God freed me from the bondage of harboring offense. Hallelujah.

You will never be bored with God's plan and will in your life. It is exciting, new, unexpected, and more desirable than you have ever dreamed and prayed for.

DAY 47

FORCE OF NATURE

Accepting Jesus Christ as your Savior means you are now a child of God going to heaven by grace through faith (See Ephesians 1:7). No one and nothing can snatch you from His hand (See John 10:28). But His grace doesn't stop there. You can use God's grace as empowerment in your everyday life here on earth, whether at work or in your family, ministries, career, hobbies, health, finances, or relationships. You can live an extraordinary life.

God, I am grateful for the revelation you gave me as I drove to Tennessee. He gave me a song titled "Until Grace" by Tauren Wells. I played the song on repeat and asked God, "who was I before your grace called me? What is the stuff inside and outside of me that grace changed?" Well, as I listened to Him, he started naming several things.

1. I returned home safely from all four Navy deployments, especially the last one from the East Coast.
2. God gave me a girlfriend and the experience of love.
3. I received healing! I can see again without glasses.
4. By His grace and because of Him, I saved over $230,000.
5. By His grace, I've been freed from the bondage of lust.
6. He granted me divine health.
7. He also freed me from legalism in my dating life.
8. By His grace, He has given me the privilege to live extraordinarily. I have realized my identity as a child of God and how much He loves me.
9. By His grace, I can set goals again and feel free to write.
10. By His grace, Henry Cloud's Boundaries and Susie Moore's Stop Checking Your Likes has helped me to enjoy life more and more and choose my friends wisely.
11. By grace, Susan Cain's book Quiet taught me about my personality as an introvert. I now appreciate being an introvert.
12. By grace, I've learned to date successfully, and that is pleasing to God.

13. Thank you, Jesus, for healing me of stomach pain. By grace, the Holy Spirit revealed that I am overeating. So, I stopped overeating, and it never happened again.
14. By His grace, He freed me from the controlling spirit of offense in dating.

FAITH connects you to unlimited empowerment of God's GRACE.

Indeed, God, Your grace is a force of nature. I didn't even know then that God was at work in all of it. Thank you, and I love you, Jesus! I encourage you to listen to Tauren Wells' song *Until Grace*.

Like I said, FAITH connects you to unlimited empowerment of God's GRACE. Let your faith be relentless, tapping into God's infinite grace in every area of your life. Keep believing in His word and promises to you, for "whatever is not from faith is sin" (Romans 14:23).

DAY 48

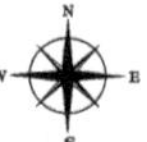

SURRENDER

Is there anything God wants you to surrender—relationship, goals, dreams, habits, time, or possessions? Are you hesitant because surrendering to Him costs you more than not surrendering? Are you confused because you don't know if the call to surrender is really from God?

"For my thoughts are not your thoughts, Nor are your ways My ways," says the LORD. "For as the heavens are higher than the earth, So are my ways higher than your ways, And my thoughts than your thoughts."

—ISAIAH 55:8-9

Charles Stanley offered valuable wisdom when he said:

God does not require us to understand His will, just obey it, even if it seems unreasonable. Even when we do not comprehend what the Lord is doing in our lives, He wants us to trust Him. His wisdom and perspective are far greater than our own. Even when we cannot discern His methods or timing, we must trust Him because His way is the best way.[44]

It is already July 7, 2022. Thank God for His extraordinary favor today in successfully delivering my medical and dental records to the hospital. I'm thankful, God, that my belongings are finally out of my apartment. Thank you, God, for a safe arrival to the house I bought, and thank you for yesterday's nap!

God's plans and dreams for your life are much better than you could ever imagine!

I'm not quite sure why, but Isaiah 55:8 is standing out to me right now. It says, "'For my thoughts *are* not your thoughts, Nor *are* your ways My ways,' says the LORD." In his sermon, my brother said, "What if letting go of everything you wanted led you to dreams you didn't know you had?" God's plans and dreams for your life are much better than you could ever imagine! Surrender to Him!

DAY 49

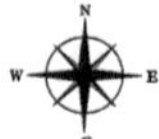

GREAT AND MIGHTY THINGS

Throughout this book, I've encouraged you to ask God to show you the great and mighty things He has done in your life, and You will be amazed at what He will show you.

Have you experienced a special someone's love, perhaps a boyfriend or a girlfriend? A bliss of emotions that satisfied your soul? I believe it was a gift from God. Even if your relationship didn't last or lead to marriage, you can still glorify God because of it, especially if you fulfilled the commandments of God to love one another (See Romans 13:8). Of course, abstaining from sex before marriage is a must.

When I first visited Nashville yesterday, I realized God blessed us mightily. My brother once rented a room to a friend he didn't like, but now he has his own house, wife, and beautiful daughter.

I joined the Navy with the rank of E-3 in the year 2005 and moved up to a seasoned first-class petty officer E-6 with 17 years of active duty service. After that, I will receive four-years free college and a pension. Through the Navy, I'm blessed to collect a housing allowance, which allowed me to buy a house to live in and invest in.

God loves to surprise His faithful people more than anything we could ever imagine.

I was on the plane, and God gave me this verse in Ephesians 3:20, "Now to Him who is able to do exceedingly abundantly above all that we ask or think, according to the power that works in us."

God loves to surprise His faithful people more than anything we could ever imagine, which is what God has done in my life. Now, I can name those surprises that never crossed my mind at the time.During my early twenties in the Navy, I had the opportunity to travel the world on sea deployments. We visited Singapore, Thailand, Australia, Jordan, Hong Kong, the Philippines, Israel, East Timor, and other exciting locations. In my thirties, I experienced the favor of God. I experienced mutual love. God's gift of being loved and loving back amazed me. As I said, God astounds me above all I could dream or think.

Thank God for the people He has brought into your life who have loved and cared for you, because love has value.

DAY 50

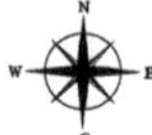

AT THE CROSS

Have you ever read a book that changed your life spiritually, financially, physically, intellectually, or relationally? Believe it or not, when you read a book, you enter into the author's mind and heart. It's like having a personal mentor who coaches you.

I owe everything to you, Jesus! I am grateful You freed me and used books to make it happen.

Let's not forget all His promises, like 1 Corinthians 2:9: "Eye has not seen, nor ear heard, nor have entered into the heart of man The things which God has prepared for those who love Him."

My friend, God, wrote a book called the Bible just for you because He cares for you.

I am scheduled to play the keyboard this week, and one of the songs on the setlist is Chris Tomlin's "At the Cross." As I sang and practiced the song, I realized that all the good and beautiful things that happened in my life started because of what Jesus did on the cross which, in turn, opens up possibilities and opportunities because of God's grace. Amen! I encourage you to listen to this song.

Imagine a life without books with messages you desperately need to hear. My friend, God, wrote a book called the Bible just for you because He cares for you. This book is His love story to you. It will protect you, make you wise, help you live an abundant life, and even answer your most significant questions in life.

DAY 51

GREAT THINGS IN STORE

You do not know the exciting things God has in store for you this coming year, but one thing is for sure: it will leave you grateful and satisfied. "Eye has not seen, nor ear heard, Nor have entered into the heart of man The things which God has prepared for those who love Him" (1 Corinthians 2:9). As you obey and remain faithful to Him, He gifts you with blessed moments that you will forever cherish, because "The memory of the righteous *is* blessed" (Proverbs 10:7).

Every new year, I write about what God has done for me the previous year. I started to ask and pray Jeremiah 33:3, "Call to me, and I will answer you, and show you great and mighty things, which you do not know."

I listened to God, and He showed me His favor of me:

1. God gave me Donnabelle as an intimate friend. She visited me here in the US twice. We talked almost every day.
2. I did what I was scared to do: send flowers to a lady named Jeremy, my crush. We talked on the phone.
3. I took some leave to visit my brother Leo, and we had fun in Florida. Also, I ate at Paula Dean's restaurant in Nashville, Tennessee with Auntie Bing and Ate Mayet. I had a blast of fun in Tennessee with them.
4. I finished reading Stop Checking Your Likes. I always wonder whether social media, like Facebook, is more destructive than it is helpful. I stumbled upon the book's last chapter about the benefits of internal validation. In summary, social media sometimes pushes us to value external validation from people who like our posts or pictures. Our decisions and moods become dependent on the acceptance of others. However, the author points out the importance of what's inside you. When you ignore your likes on Facebook, you become true to yourself.[45] Applying this to my life has allowed me to be more intimate with God without social media distractions.
5. Lastly, I learned from Dr. Keith Johnson to declare, "I decree and declare that an elephant-sized relationship will come into my life," and "I decree

and declare that you will make our name great, for God's glory."[46] I started meeting people who favored or pushed me to improve just by speaking these declarations. Thank you, Jesus.

Last night, as I worshiped God, He revealed what has He accomplished over the years and what He has planned next. It amazes me how He does things—His ways never cross or enter my mind as a possible path forward. Just the thought of it leaves me very grateful and in awe of His wonders.

He also led me to Isaiah 64:4. I could see and picture the verse, "For since the beginning of the world Men have not heard nor perceived by the ear, Nor has the eye seen any God besides You, Who acts for the one who waits for Him."

2018: I met my ex-girlfriend and experienced love.

2020: I stayed in Great Lakes, Illinois. I got to live in a hotel for six months and just go to school. It was like a vacation! I also found a church and community. I tried different kinds of delicious food and enjoyed driving from Chicago, to Tennessee, to Virginia.

2021: I deployed and visited Egypt/Israel. Because of that deployment, I was able to save for closing on my house ($10,000). God also gave me friendship with two faithful friends, Rob and Kaleb. We enjoy playing and learning music. I've also started dating Donnabelle.

2022: I bought a house and enjoyed dating Donnabelle and Nguyen at the beginning of the year. Before the year's end, I joined ReGenesis Church Christmas caroling. I enjoyed the fellowship and opportunity to sharpen my piano skills. I tried different kinds of food and grew closer to God. I felt the same favor when I found the Berean Fundamental Baptist Church in Great Lakes, Illinois.

Charles Stanley says,

The richest moments in life are not the most expensive. Often they are the cheapest—the laughter of a child, a hug from a grandparent, a cup of coffee with a friend, a fishing trip with Dad, an "I love you" from Mom. The next time you find yourself wishing you had more, ask God to show you how rich you really are in Him.[47]

DAY 52

HE WILL SHOW YOU THE PATH

If you want to know God's will for your life and seek it with all your heart, He will reveal it to you. Sometimes, it's not about how you want to hear it, where you will hear it, or what you want to hear. God has His own way of speaking to you.

"For since the beginning of the world Men have not heard nor perceived by the ear,
Nor has the eye seen any God besides You, who acts for the one who waits for Him."
—ISAIAH 64:4

I waited and prayed for clarity on what God wanted me to pursue: a bachelor of science in nursing or a bachelor's in general study. I asked Him for a Bible verse and got 2 Kings 7:3, "Now there were four leprous men at the entrance of the gate; and they said to one another, 'Why are we sitting here until we die?'"

Next time you have a minor or significant question, let God know, and He will take care of the rest.

In Dr. Keith Johnson's sermon, God wants us to decide and start the first step, whether it's toward our dream, desire, or in pursuit of something else God tells us to do. I am listening to God, and He told me to go ahead and pursue nursing—my dream—and He promised He would help me. He paid for my schooling, helped me in my classes, and ultimately enabled me to graduate as a nurse. Thank you, Jesus.

Next time you have a minor or significant question, let God know, and He will take care of the rest.

"Trust in the LORD with all your heart, And lean not on your own understanding;
In all your ways acknowledge Him, And He shall direct your paths."
—PROVERBS 3:5-6

DAY 53

GOD WITHIN AND AMONG US

God has more new things for you every minute, day, and year. He has more and more for you because He wants you to feel joy, satisfaction, and peace. He has more ideas to share with you, more expressions of love to shower upon you, and an unlimited supply of new accomplishments, new mercies, new blessings, and new inspirations.

God still wants me to enjoy life as a single man. He is not done with me yet! He wants me to travel, like when I lived in Chicago. God guaranteed that I would be amazed and rejoice over His favor. He is about to do something exceptional and remarkable.

"The LORD bless you and keep you; The LORD make His face shine upon you, And be gracious to you; The LORD lift up His countenance upon you, And give you peace."

—Numbers 6:24-26

Lord, Your extraordinary favor amazes me. It is almost the end of the year. I am enjoying life because of it. Your gift of favor advances me exponentially into beautiful moments. Sister Ellen always reminds me that I will surpass the blessings of my brothers. As I dwell in God's presence, He gave me a song titled "The Blessing" by Cody Carnes, Kari Jobe, and Elevation Worship. Blessing is the theme of my year. During my broken months, God's love has sustained me. According to Pastor Steven Furtick, breaking produces a blessing because God promises to dwell among and within broken and contrite hearts.[48] That means when we are heartbroken, we must abide in God's love to experience His presence in greater measure.

On August 1st, I wondered what would happen to me if I was assigned to a ship or deployed. God reminded me that knowing who is with you is more important than knowing where you're going.

Today, I'm reminded of Joshua 1:9, "Have I not commanded you? Be strong and of good courage; do not be afraid, nor be dismayed, for the LORD your God is with you wherever you go."

As Stanley stated,

God has promised to be with us. When we face trials of any kind, He is beside us. When we experience joy, love, and sorrow, He is close to us. Nothing is greater than Him, and He has pledged never to leave us. The only way we hinder the victory is through disobedience and unbelief. So no matter what you are facing or how bad your situation seems, take courage, believe Him, and do exactly as He says. With Him fighting for you, there's absolutely no reason to be afraid.[49]

DAY 54

PERFECT TIMING

"To everything there is a season, A time for every purpose under heaven. . . . He has made everything beautiful in its time."
—ECCLESIASTES 3:1, 11

Have you ever felt like everything is crumbling, and you are left emotionally broken? Then, the next thing you know, everything is coming back into place and in your favor. You feel love and emotional healing again.

God is the one who can turn our pain and messiness into something beautiful.

I was worshiping here in the hotel, enjoying the beach view, when God spoke to me. He told me He put me in a hotel for six months with thirty days off to mourn, pray, relax, listen to Him, make mistakes, enjoy life, and fellowship with others because He knew about my brokenness beforehand. God was still with me in my brokenness when I felt I was falling apart. He embraced and comforted me. Thank you, Jesus!

When you don't see any hope because the pain of brokenness has consumed you, trust God. The old saying is somewhat true: "Time heals all wounds." He uses time for everything! God is the one who can turn our pain and messiness into something beautiful.

DAY 55

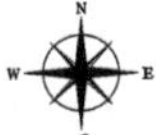

HIGHLY INVESTED

Whether you know it or not, God invests so much in you! He gave you your life and family, showered you with love from all sources, and supplied all your needs. It is like an investor putting his money in the stock market because he knows there's potential for growth.

Lord, time and time again, I am grateful for Your extraordinary favor in my life. "I am more than a conqueror who walks in the extraordinary favor of God and man" (See Romans 8:37). Lord, during my leave, I reflected on my life and saw that Your favor and presence were evident. You've shown me the marvelous work You've done for me. Thank you, Jesus.

After I believed back in 2015 that God would show me extraordinary favor through grace, my life changed. My life has become an adventure. I love you, Lord. Blessing after blessing, favor after favor.

Steven Furtick wrote,

One Sunday, we spent some time with Holly Furtick, reflecting back on how God saw us through 2020. It turns out, when you take time to look back, you can trace the favor of God on your life every step of the way. It's evident that God's presence has been with us every step of the way.[50]

I am the LORD your God, Who brought you out of the land of Egypt; Open your mouth wide, and I will fill it.

—PSALM 81:10

According to Charles Stanley, "Here, we see the heart of God: He desires to bless His people beyond their imaginations. But we also see our part in the process: to willingly receive what He has to offer by submitting ourselves to Him. We are filled only when we obey His instructions."[51]

He values and loves you so much that He will pay that much—the cost of His son's life, Jesus Christ. God has invested so much in me. Thank You for Your word in Psalm 81:10.

Not only has God invested in you, but He has also bought you at a very high price. He values and loves you so much that He will pay that much—the cost of His son's life, Jesus Christ.

"For you were bought at a price; therefore glorify God in your body and in your spirit, which are God's."

—1 CORINTHIANS 6:20

"Those who trust in their wealth And boast in the multitude of their riches, None of them can by any means redeem his brother, Nor give to God a ransom for him—For the redemption of their soul is costly, And it shall cease forever."

—PSALM 49:6-8

DAY 56

BLESSED FUTURE

When you obey and stay faithful to God, He blesses and protects everything you own, including your savings and finances. According to Psalm 107:38, "He also blesses them, and they multiply greatly; And He does not let their cattle decrease."

Last night, God spoke to me in a mighty way. I remember singing "Give Thanks" by Steffany Gretzinger and Melissa Helser back in the Philippines. It goes like this: "Let the weak say I am strong; let the poor say I am rich."[52] Then I asked God, "How could the children of God in the Philippines like me, who barely make it, be rich?" His answer was clear—"through Me—the God of the universe, to whom riches, honor, and fame belong!" Thank you, Jesus! As I worship, God reminds me how He has blessed me with a wealth of $200,000. That is approximately 8 million pesos in Philippine money.

I pray that God bless you mightily and grants the desires of your heart.

"Both riches and honor come from You, And You reign over all. In Your hand is power and might; In Your hand it is to make great And to give strength to all."

—1 CHRONICLES 29:12

Three years ago, Sister Ellen prophesied that God would give me honor and fame. She said that I would finish my master's degree and excel in three things.

"Though your beginning was small, Yet your latter end would increase abundantly."

—JOB 8:7

As you read this devotion, I pray that God bless you mightily and grants the desires of your heart. I renounce and destroy any spirit of lack and debt and speak abundance, prosperity, and financial breakthroughs over your life. In Jesus' name, I pray. Amen!

DAY 57

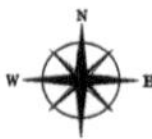

THANK GOD YOU OBEYED

"Why do you spend money for what is not bread, And your wages for what does not satisfy? Listen carefully to Me, and eat what is good, And let your soul delight itself in abundance."
—ISAIAH 55:2

Dr. Charles Stanley said, "To obey God is to bless yourself; to disobey Him is to curse yourself."[53] Jesus said, "I have come that they may have life, and that they may have *it* more abundantly" (John 10:10). I thank God for guiding me on what to do about Ms. Delsey and other women I dated back in Chicago. As I have obeyed Him, His favor has showered over me.

Who knows how many times He has shielded and saved you from danger?

When you do what the Holy Spirit prompts you to do, God will put a hedge of protection around you. His instructions are for your benefit. Who knows how many times He has shielded and saved you from danger?

The fear of the Lord is the key to obedience, even if you don't see its benefits or it doesn't make sense. Your awe and fear of the Lord will guide your decision and motivate you to do what He wants.

"Then the man said, 'The woman whom You gave to be with me, she gave me of the tree, and I ate.'"
—GENESIS 3:12

Lately, God has been pointing me to the story of Adam and Eve. When God told me not to get back together with my ex-girlfriend, Kelsey, I hesitated but obeyed. Like

Adam, who ate the apple and blamed Eve, I could have disobeyed God and blamed Kelsey, but I knew that God would hold me accountable for my actions. I could have justified my actions, that I returned to Kelsey because I was confused or because I still loved her and she still loved me, but disobedience to Him always leads to regret, deeper emotional pain, and more broken relationships.

Stay on the path of obedience and develop the fear of the Lord that fuels it.

There is a sense of joy right now in my heart that God gave me the wisdom and courage to obey Him and not return to my ex-girlfriend. His favor and blessing immediately followed my obedience.

Stanley states, "Sin impels us to blame others for our disobedience and folly, but God holds us personally accountable for what we do."[54] Imagine a wave of joy, peace, and a clear conscience bubble up inside of you. These are only a few of the benefits of obeying God. Stay on the path of obedience and develop the fear of the Lord that fuels it.

DAY 58

BOOKS ARE A PATHWAY TO HIM

Believe it or not, you will always have a great mentor, friend, Comforter, wise Counselor, coach, cheerleader, and therapist in God. As children of God, we are never alone (See Joshua 1:9; Hebrews 13:5). The Holy Spirit is living inside you. Sometimes, you just need to tap into your greatest Resource—the Holy Spirit—for help. Other times, He will lead and teach you without your requesting a thing.

I feel grateful that Jesus Christ and the Holy Spirit changed my life through books. They have turned my life and walk around 180 degrees.

2008: I was twenty-two years old when I read Joshua Harris' *Not Even a Hint*. God freed me from the bondage of lust through this book. Through the grace of God, ordinary people like you and me can walk in holiness.

2013: God gave me wisdom at twenty-seven years old about how to best take care of my body after reading Dr. Don Colbert's *Toxic Relief*. Thank you, Jesus! God also blessed me financially and taught me biblical financial stewardship. I love you, God, for using my brother to open my eyes with Dave Ramsey's *Total Money Makeover*.

2015: My life has completely changed as He has taken me from glory to glory. At twenty-nine years old, I'm a changed man emotionally, financially, physically, and spiritually. Life became more exciting after I read John Bevere's *Extraordinary*.

"This resurrection life you received from God is not a timid, grave-tending life. It's adventurously expectant, greeting God with a childlike 'What's next, Papa?'"

—ROMANS 8:15-17 (MSG)

God has imparted life, blessing, and favor onto me. Thank you, Jesus! I genuinely grasp the promises of John 10:10, "I have come that you may have life and life abundantly"—a great full life. A rich and satisfying life. A life at its fullness.

2018: I am completely free from the bondage of legalism in dating. Thank you, Holy Spirit, for leading me to Dr. Henry Cloud and Dr. John Townsend's *Boundaries in Dating*.

One thing is sure: what He's doing or saying to you is very important, life-changing, and for your benefit!

The Holy Spirit could direct you using other people, books, God's Word, and your circumstances, to name a few. One thing is sure: what He's doing or saying to you is very important, life-changing, and for your benefit! So, you better take heed.

DAY 59

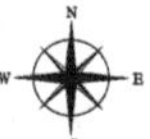

EMOTIONAL CONNECTION

We sometimes tend to fit God around our dating life instead of our dating life around God. We need to aim for the latter, because our desires and feelings are all part of His grand creation.

God gave me this verse while standing Under Instruction (U/I) with my mentee: "Every good and perfect gift is from above, coming down from the Father of the heavenly lights, who does not change like shifting shadows" (James 1:17, NIV).

I felt the abundant blessing of God showered on me as my joy and gratitude turned into praise. Thank you, Lord. Then, I asked God what He wanted to say through this verse. He said life and love are His domain. He is most capable of forging emotional connection and intimacy (in a friendship, romantic relationship, or marriage) that will satisfy me and glorify His great name.

When you find and pursue your dreams,
the intimacy will follow.

Seth Godin's review of Michael Hyatt's *Your Best Year Ever* stood out to me: "Generous goals work (if you write them down) and powerful books work (if you read them). Michael Hyatt has created a fun, fast way to find your dreams and then turn them into reality."[55] When you find and pursue your dreams, the intimacy will follow.

Submit and surrender everything to God, including your dating life. Acknowledge Him in all your dating decisions. God can satisfy your need for love.

"For in Him we live and move and have our being."
–ACT 17:28

DAY 60

WORTH THE WAIT

Sometimes, the best thing in life is the one you waited for the most. Through waiting, you allow God to work on your behalf.

"Better a handful with quietness Than both hands full,
together with toil and grasping for the wind."
—ECCLESIASTES 4:6

Charles Stanley said:

Paul wrote, "Godliness with contentment is great gain" (1 Tim. 6:6). In other words, when we submit to God—resting in Him and trusting Him to take care of the consequences of our obedience—He supplies everything we need. Therefore, we should find all of our joy and fulfillment in Him. Those who walk closely with God can learn to be content in whatever circumstances arise. Paul said he had "learned both to be full and to be hungry, both to abound and to suffer need" (Phil. 4:12).[56]

When you find yourself in the waiting process, view it as an opportunity to experience the best thing in life.

Lately, God has given me verse after verse in Ecclesiastes, including the verse opening today's devotional. As I read it, God impressed me with the mighty things He has done in Great Lakes, Illinois. As I wait on the blessing of obedience while I'm there, He supplies all my needs. Waiting itself is a blessing. During my time in Illinois, He did exceedingly and abundantly above all that I could have asked or thought, things far above my wildest dreams or expectations. He has assured me that He will do the same while I'm stationed in this command (USS Monterey) and during deployment.

When you find yourself in the waiting process, view it as an opportunity to experience the best things in life. As Charles Stanley said, "Don't run ahead of God's timing! His blessings are always worth the wait."[57]

DAY 61

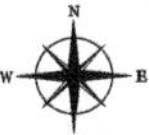

THE VERY BEST

Doesn't "the very best" sound pretty nice? Everyone, including you, wishes to be their best version and experience the best of everything in life.

Today, I am happy I am well-rested and not on the watchbill again (a watchbill is a list of responsibilities given to a Sailor to man or watch at a particular time and location inside the ship.) I'm grateful I have free time today to do what I want. I like to share Isaiah 30:18 today:

"Therefore the LORD will wait, that He may be gracious to you; And therefore He will be exalted, that He may have mercy on you. For the LORD is a God of justice; Blessed are all those who wait for Him."

I have asked God to tell me the very best things He has done for me. For starters, I have one of the best jobs in the Navy here in the US. I was meant to go to this deployment and can stay in a nice hotel by the beach for three days. I also rode in the helicopter. Wow, now THAT is an experience. Even in deployment, I can seek the mentorship of others and serve God with music alongside Chaplain Friebel.

I reviewed day 59's "Emotional Connection" journal entry when God spoke to me. He said He would satisfy my emotional longing for love and intimacy in a way that would amaze and satisfy me so that I may give Him all the glory. I won't regret waiting because the Lord is waiting, too—to release His best blessing to me. He is perfecting the blessing.

There are many other "very best things" that have come from God:

- » I have the best brothers.
- » I have the best church, ministries, community group, and faithful friends.
- » I live in one of the best cities, Virginia Beach.
- » I get to taste the best food.
- » I have the best hobbies and get to read the best books.
- » I have the best lifestyle, like an apartment, car, and clothing, and I'm still single, not worrying about anything or anyone else.
- » I have the best job (stable with full benefits like a pension and retirement.)

Thank You for all of these things, God. Indeed, life is worth living because You live. "My purpose is to give them a rich and satisfying life" (John 10:10, NLT).

My friend, I have a simple answer: Obey God in everything.

God is also giving me a random flashback as I write. A while back, God told me through His prophet Sister Ellen that I would live a high, first-class life. She said that He would give me the best anointing, favor, and everything. I am experiencing it even now.

If you're asking, "How can I live and experience the very best God has for me?" My friend, I have a simple answer: Obey God in everything. Nothing is more straightforward than that because obedience always brings blessings.

DAY 62

VICTORY

When you acknowledge or ask the Lord for guidance, He will direct you. You may not hear His voice now, but your willingness to listen, wait, and obey will put you in a favorable position for victory. As you seek His guidance, He will orchestrate a series of events to elevate your situation under His protection.

"The works of righteousness will be peace, and the effect of righteousness, quietness and assurance forever."

—ISAIAH 32:17

"You have seen what I did to the Egyptians, and how I bore you on eagles' wings and brought you to Myself. Now therefore, if you will indeed obey My voice and keep my covenant, then you shall be a special treasure to Me above all the people; for all the earth is Mine."

—EXODUS 19:4-5

"Victory" is the Word God has given me today. He will give me victory in the command. I will get my Enlisted Surface Warfare Specialist (ESWS) requalification and become a qualified Electrical Plant Control Console (EPCC). He will help me accomplish all my goals. Thank you, Jesus. I will be satisfied with my tour on the USS Monterey ship (CG–61).

God is speaking to me about the story of David. David always asked God to direct his steps wherever he went and whenever it was time to fight.

"So David inquired of the LORD, saying, 'Shall I go up against the Philistines? Will you deliver them into my hands?' And the LORD said to David, 'Go up, for I will doubtless deliver the Philistines into your hands.'"

—2 SAMUEL 5:19

Stanley says, "As long as David asked for the Lord's guidance, he enjoyed success. When he stopped listening to the Lord's voice, he landed in trouble. The same is true for us."[58]

Make a habit out of bringing every decision to God.

While I was on watch earlier today, God reminded me of His promise that there would be no casualties throughout my whole stay here on the ship. Since we left deployment, there has been no class C fire. Someone also proficiently took over SKED and AWN (software for maintenance and ordering parts) to help me. Thank you, Jesus. You have thoroughly given me greatness, peace, rest, and assurance forever. Now, I'm working on my EPCC. As God promised, I will become a qualified engineering officer of the watch (EOOW), engineering duty officer (EDO), and damage control training team member (DCTT). Hallelujah! Thank you for Psalm 127:1:

"Unless the LORD builds the house, They labor in vain who build it; Unless the LORD guards the city, The watchman stays awake in vain."

Just like King David, make a habit out of bringing every decision to God. It will lead to victory and safety every single time.

DAY 63

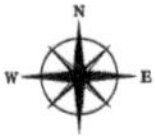

LOVE IS A CHOICE

There will be times in your relationships when you will not understand yourself, your feelings, and the other person. The more a relationship grows, the more it becomes vulnerable to pain.

"Give, and it will be given to you: good measure, pressed down, shaken together, and running over will be put into your bosom. For with the same measure that you use, it will be measured back to you."

—LUKE 6:38

Well, here we go again with my dating lessons. Whenever I was mad at my ex-girlfriend, Kelsey, I would ask myself whether I should follow my emotions. If I didn't, it seemed I was being dishonest with myself and her. Gary Chapman said that love is a choice.[59] I should have chosen not to follow my anger and instead love her for her benefit. In future relationships, I will decide to give just like the verse in Luke 6:38 commands.

As Chapman best explains:

If you claim to have feelings you do not have, that is hypocritical and such false communication is not the way to build intimate relationships. But if you express an act of love designed for the other person's benefit or pleasure, it's simply a choice. You are not claiming the action grows out of a deep emotional bonding. You are simply choosing to do something for his benefit. I think that must be what Jesus meant.[60]

In addition, you'll find great reward from choosing to love. Luke 6:35 says: "But love your enemies, do good, and lend, hoping for nothing in return; and your reward will be great, and you will be sons of the Most High." I guess that must have been another cure for my controlling attitude.

Chapman also said, "Certainly we do not have warm feelings for people who hate us. That would be abnormal, but we can do loving acts for them. That is simply a choice."[61] Thank you, Jesus!

DAY 64

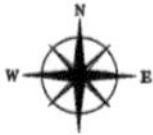

OBEDIENCE ALWAYS LEADS TO BLESSING

You've probably noticed that this book focuses heavily on obedience to God and gratitude for His works through examples of great characters in the Bible and my personal experiences. This is intentional—I chose to retain these repetitive themes to preserve their honesty and authenticity. Our obedience is not only paramount to receive all of God's blessings but it's also critical for the people closest to us.

"He who heeds the word wisely will find good, and
whoever trusts in the LORD, happy is he."
—PROVERBS 16:20

Charles Stanley says, "No one will ever find true happiness by disobeying a clear command of God. Our joy is found in trusting the Lord and becoming all He created us to be. Those who disobey show that they do not truly trust that He has their best interest at heart."[62]

Lately, God has given me a word regarding the importance of obeying Him. Thank you, Jesus. Just the simple act of obedience can change our destiny because it always leads to blessings. There is great value in obedience. It has taken a few days for me to discern what God is speaking this week.

I've been asking God what to do every time I need to make an important decision, and it always produces tremendous results. One of the verses He gave me is from 2 Samuel 5:10, which states, "So David went on and became great, and the LORD God of hosts was with him." According to Charles Stanley, "When we follow the Lord wholeheartedly as David did, we too, will enjoy His wonderful presence. And just as He did with David, He can cause us to grow in godliness and even to become great for the sake of His kingdom."[63] As I obey, He will make me great for the sake of His glory and Kingdom.

Around the first week of June 2021, God promised to make me fruitful to fulfill His purpose for my life. He also promised to assume full responsibility for my needs and heart's desires as I obey Him. I will have a whole and full life. Henry Cloud said, "The by-product of fullness is that the fulfilled person is also a very attractive one."[64]

As I write, the Holy Spirit has given me Genesis 24:1 which states, "Now Abraham was old, well advanced in age; and the LORD had blessed Abraham in all things." Stanley asked an important question as it pertains to this Scripture, "Would you like to be blessed in every way as Abraham was? Then you must follow Abraham's example of trust and obedience, for that is the way to great blessings."[65]

Reading this Scripture showered me with an unexplainable deep peace and joy. I would not trade any of it for what this world has to offer. I love you, Jesus. That was precisely what happened when I was in Great Lakes, Illinois, and in this deployment. Thank you, Jesus!

Charles Stanley remarks:

When we live obedient lives, those who know and love us will sense the peace and joy He has given us. Instead of conflict, there will be contentment—and that is just one part of experiencing God's goodness. When you choose to obey the Lord, He will bless you. This is because obedience always leads to blessing. I have always told people who say they do not understand why God is asking them to do a certain thing that if they obey Him, He will reward them with a sense of peace and joy that compares to nothing this world has to offer. Therefore, set a goal to obey the Lord and watch Him work in your life.[66]

DAY 65

UNCERTAIN WORLD

You are living in a world of uncertainty. We don't know who our next president will be or what our economy will look like next year, yet you have a Father who will always be on your side, knows everything, and is dedicated to protecting and caring for you.

"I will give you the rain for your land in its season, the early rain and the latter rain."
—DEUTERONOMY 11:14

Stanley says,

Throughout Israel's history, its success or failure hinged on two short rainy seasons. The early rains, which occurred in the fall, would soften the ground for planting and nourishing the seeds. The late rains replenished the crops before the heat of summer. Everything depended on the precipitation—if all went well, there would be plenty of crops. If it did not, there would be famine and devastation. Our God provides for those who love Him and who obey His commandments. In today's uncertain world, it's good to be in the hands of our loving God, who knows what we need before we even ask Him for it.[67]

As the ship fixed the Collection, Holding, and Transfer (CHT), a system that handles human waste, some people couldn't shower. Thank God I've got wipes and can shower quickly. I recovered from my sleep even though I had a watch last night. Thank you also for helping me with my watch, Jesus, and sending people to assist me. Amid my uncertain schedule, God has told me that we don't know when or how to fix something, but He does. He reminds me that being by His side and obeying Him are good; they keep us safe and send favor and blessing to us because He knows what we desire before asking.

Staying on God's side and constantly walking in His perfect will will always benefit you!

Honestly, it is scary to think that someone do not even know Jesus Christ yet live in this unpredictable world. Staying on God's side and constantly walking in His perfect will will always benefit you!

DAY 66

GOD'S BEST

Since God's plan for us is always the best, I want to define the word *"BEST."* According to the Thesaurus.com, its synonyms are finest, first, leading, outstanding, perfect, and terrific.[68] Dictionary.com's select definitions of "best" include:

Adjective

- » Of the highest quality, excellence, or standing
- » Most advantageous, suitable, or desirable

Adverb

- » Most excellently or suitably; with most advantage or success
- » In or to the highest degree; most fully

Noun

- » The best, something or someone that is the most excellent, most suitable, of the highest quality, or the highest degree
- » A person's most agreeable or desirable emotional state[69]

Don't throw away God's best for your life for the fleeting pleasure of sin or anything the devil offers.

Each definition describes what God has planned and what He has in store for you. Isn't that wonderful? Don't throw away God's best for your life for the fleeting pleasure of sin or anything the devil offers. Keep following God!

"Guard your heart above all else, for it determines the course of your life."
—PROVERBS 4:23 (NLT)

DAY 67

GOD'S GUIDANCE

Different people have different perspectives and points of view. Often, they give advice based on their own experience, beliefs, or what they learn from others. But sometimes, you need access to the right people and resources at the right time. The Holy Spirit, your wise companion, is dependable and available 24/7.

"But I say to the unmarried and to the widows: It is good for them if they remain even as I am."
–1 CORINTHIANS 7:8

According to Charles Stanley,

Many times people rush into marriage because they long for security, acceptance, companionship, and love. They also yearn to be like others in society. However, making any decisions without God's guidance can be devastating—especially one like marriage that affects the rest of your life. Therefore in marriage—just as everything else—remember that God's plan for your life is best, and He acts on behalf of those who wait for Him.[70]

He has probably saved me from a ton of heartache that comes with unhealthy relationships just from asking for His guidance first.

One day, I helped a pretty lady with an electrical safety check for her personal equipment. I asked God if I should ask her out on a date. The Holy Spirit promptly answered my question because the lady confessed (without me even asking about her personal life) that she was divorced and lost everything after the incident. As soon as she shared that, I decided it was best not to ask her on a date. How many divorces could have been avoided if we had only listened and obeyed God's guidance?

I thank God for answering my question. He has probably saved me from a ton of heartache that comes with unhealthy relationships just from asking for His guidance first. It's a relief that I've avoided heartbreak, wasted time, and wasted money. Amen! Thank you, Jesus, for only giving me a fulfilling romantic relationship.

The next time you need advice, ask the Holy Spirit. He will answer you because He lives inside you.

"God is our refuge and strength, A very present help in trouble."
—PSALM 46:1

However, when He, the Spirit of truth, has come, He will guide you into all truth; for He will not speak on His own authority, but whatever He hears He will speak; and He will tell you things to come.
—JOHN 16:13

DAY 68

YOU ARE WELCOME

When you accept Jesus Christ as your personal Savior, you become a child of God. He always welcomes and loves you. I listened to Pastor Robert's sermon titled "Recognize Your True Identity in Christ" this morning on YouTube. I've learned that your identity is a child of God and being a child of God is the highest calling you could ever have.

My wounds are already healed after a long vacation due to my Sick in Quarters (SIQ). The doctor gave me six days off and two weeks of Light Limited Duty (LLD). I am so thankful to God for having that day off because I have plenty of time to pray, read His word, and study for my accounting class assignment. So far, I have passed the assignments, quizzes, and midterm with flying colors. My classmates and I met today to finish our homework, and I really learned a lot.

Thank you, Jesus. The real reason why I wanted to chat and write today is because of what's going on at my work. As I returned to work this Wednesday, all my coworkers welcomed me. They asked me, with great concern, what happened to my foot. I told them that I spilled hot tea on it. Many coworkers were concerned and cared for me when I was injured. It was so nice to see EM2 Tyrell again. We talked and shook hands; it had been a while since we had seen each other. I appreciate the time to fully recover. I praise my awesome God.

I'll leave you with a quote by Charlie Jones, "Five years from today, you'll be the same person you are except for the books you read and the people you meet."

DAY 69

FAITH AND HUMILITY

Did you know that exercising your faith is a true sign of humility? "Behold the proud, His soul is not upright in him; But the just shall live by his faith" (Habakkuk 2:4). Humility and faith go hand in hand, as do pride and unbelief. Having faith means trusting God instead of relying on yourself, which is humility. On the other hand, a lack of faith shows you would rather trust yourself than trust God's wisdom and power, which is pride in disguise.

God, I am thankful for all the books I've read, including John Bevere's *Relentless*. I am learning valuable lessons and increasing my faith. For example, John Bevere compares our redemption through Jesus' sacrifice on the cross to the Israelites redemption from the Egyptians. I had never really thought about that before.

"Remember this day in which you went out of Egypt, out of the house of bondage; for by strength of hand the LORD brought you out of this place" (Exodus 13:3). Yet the Israelites forgot God and His promise to deliver them from the Canaanites and bring them to the promised land. The hard part was done—He had freed His people from Egypt's bondage.

When God gives you a word and a promise of blessing, hold it tightly and have faith because it will come to pass.

John Bevere said,

God mightily "rescued us from the domain of darkness and brought us into the kingdom of the Son whom He loves" (Colossians 1:13, GNT). If He accomplished this impossible feat, how much more can He handle far less complex and difficult situations in our lives, like healing sickness and disease, providing for our needs, granting us wisdom, and empowering us to be set apart and overcome. "Impossible" odds. Let's not repeat Israel's folly and soon forget His works (See Psalms 106:13). Let's stay clothed in the armor of humility as Caleb and Joshua did.[71]

During the last underway, I lost my Navy ID. I prayed to God and claimed His promises in Lamentation 3:22-23, "Through the LORD's mercies we are not consumed, because His compassions fail not. They are new every morning; Great is your faithfulness" and in Psalm 46:1, "God is our refuge and strength, a very present help in trouble."

After a few days of praying and fasting, My ID miraculously appeared. It would have been such a hassle if I had lost my ID; I would have had to route a request chit that I needed a new one, and there is a chance they would not have issued it to me because of my expired driver's license. Another sailor would have had to escort me every day to get to the ship.

But thanks to God, I didn't lose my ID. I love you, Jesus, for helping me find much of my stuff. I give you all the glory, honor, and praise.

When God gives you a word and a promise of blessing, hold it tightly and have faith because it will come to pass. "But the ones that fell on the good ground are those who, having heard the word with noble and good heart, keep it and bear fruit with patience" (Luke 8:15).

DAY 70

JOY

"For God gives wisdom and knowledge and joy to a man who is good in His sight."
—ECCLESIASTES 2:26

"You will show me the path of life; In Your presence is fullness of joy; At Your right hand are pleasure forevermore."
—PSALM 16:11

"Rejoice in the Lord always. Again, I will say, rejoice!"
—PHILIPPIANS 4:4

If you are like me and grew up as a Christian and attended numerous churches, you have at some point questioned what and who to believe. Knowing God's Word and keeping your joy intact is critical to avoid falling into man-made rules and legalism that sometimes steal our happiness. Read Colossians 2:20-23:

Therefore, if you died with Christ from the basic principles of the world, why, as though living in the world, do you subject yourselves to regulations—"Do not touch, do not taste, do not handle," which all concern things which perish with the using—according to the commandments and doctrines of men? These things indeed have an appearance of wisdom in self-imposed religion, false humility, and neglect of the body, but are of no value against the indulgence of the flesh.

My brother posted this on Facebook, "Your joy is critical. If you maintain your joy, you win."[72] Through his post, God spoke to me to rejoice no matter my situation, especially with my parents. God will solve my problems and deliver me from affliction. I will rejoice because God redeems me from the darkness. He showers me with loving kindness and tender mercy (See Psalm 103:4).

God isn't scrutinizing your actions or investigating your motives to condemn you.

God continues to warn me against living in legalism. God is not a legalist. Instead, he wants me to live in grace. Consider John 3:17, "For God did not send his Son into the world to condemn the world, but that the world through him might be saved" and James 2:13, "Mercy triumphs over judgment."

"And you shall know the truth, and the truth shall make you free. . . .
Therefore, if the son makes you free, you shall be free indeed."
—JOHN 8:32, 36

God isn't scrutinizing your actions or investigating your motives to condemn you. Instead, Jesus says He came to set you free.

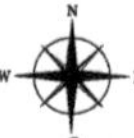

A SAILOR'S FINAL WORD

Thank you for allowing me to share insights that I have learned from my walk with God. As I previously mentioned, this book has been twenty-five years in the making. Here's what I hope you take away from it:

1. God's grace empowers us to live extraordinarily in this world, and God delights when we do. He paid a high price for us, not just to be ordinary but to excel and be the best representation of His glory.
2. We also tackled the value of waiting; we will experience the best God has for us when we wait. It's just the reality of His nature (See Isaiah 64:4).
3. We demonstrated the importance of journaling and reading. This book was quickly made possible because of that habit. Journaling enables you to learn from your past and helps you to be authentic with yourself, others, and God. It will also give you joy, hope, and a sense of purpose.
4. God is greater than your sin. Only through the power of God's grace and the cross of Jesus Christ can we be freed from the bondage of lust.
5. We should prioritize obedience to God because it always leads to blessings.
6. Living and walking in your identity in Christ pleases Him. The Bible is full of encouragement about who we really are as children of God. There is no room for insecurity when we know our identity in Christ. We are always loved, favored, and forgiven.
7. There are benefits to hardship and trials. The painful events of our lives are not worth comparing to what we gain afterward: increased wisdom, strength, rulership, authority, utility to the Kingdom, and more. We are heirs of God (See Romans 8:16-18). As heirs, everything belongs to you (See 1 Corinthians 3:21). According to John Bevere,

Everything is yours, including the world, life, death, the present, and the future. Everything belongs to you. Stop and ponder this for a day or two. In Christ, you and I are far richer than the world's richest man! [73]

8. Faith is the pipeline that allows you to access the unlimited grace of God in every area of your life.
9. Dream big and set audacious goals.

I'd like to emphasize one more thing. Setting audacious goals and dreams is important because it develops our faith and grows us. God delights in granting our requests, both big and small. He is a God without limitations.

"Now to Him who is able to do exceedingly abundantly above all that we ask or think, according to the power that works in us."
—EPHESIANS 3:19

The difference between a believer and a non-believer of Jesus Christ who sets dreams and goals is that a believer of Christ acknowledges God first in pursuing his or her goals and dreams, and they deeply care about whether those desires and dreams are congruent with the will of God. True success is not merely about accomplishing our goals and dreams. True success is about achieving our *biggest* goals and dreams, which align with the perfect will of God. Dr. Keith Johnson states, "Success starts with understanding and fulfilling my God-given assignment. I can have goals, but if I achieve things God didn't call me to do, I am a failure."[74]

Lastly, I have shared with you many stories of my past and how I struggled with lust, but I have yet to tell you how I got out of it. It's not a secret. I've mentioned the grace of God repeatedly. That's what the book is all about. I relied on the grace of God and the power of the cross of Jesus Christ and found victory over it, and you can too. God loves you too much to make it overly complicated, and He wants you to be free from it.

"God testified concerning him: 'I have found David son of Jesse, a man after my own heart; he will do everything I want him to do'... Now when David had served God's purpose in his own generation, he fell asleep."
—ACTS 13:22, 36 (NIV)

I hope you have learned valuable insights into the character and heart of God. May God bless you mightily, and may you serve God's purpose in your own generation.

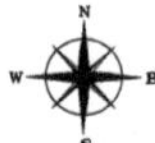

APPENDIX

BOOK RECOMMENDATION LIST

John Bevere

1. Breaking Intimidation
2. Extraordinary

Bob Burg and David Mann

3. The Go-Giver

Susan Cain

4. Quiet

Sam Chand

5. Leadership Pain

Gary Chapman

6. Things I Wish I'd Known Before We Got Married
7. The 5 Love Languages

Henry Cloud and John Townsend

8. Boundaries
9. Boundaries in Dating
10. Boundaries for Leaders
11. The Power of the Other

Don Colbert

12. Living in Divine Health
13. Toxic Relief
14. The Seven Pillars of Health
15. What You Don't Know May Be Killing You

Maury Davis

16. The Last Ride

DC Talk

17. Jesus Freaks

Elisabeth Elliot

18. Passion and Purity

Jentezen Franklin

19. Fasting

Ryan Frederick

20. Right Place, Right Time

Joshua Harris

21. I Kissed Dating Goodbye
22. Boy Meets Girl
23. Stop Dating the Church
24. Not Even a Hint

Benny Hinn

25. Good morning, Holy Spirit
26. Welcome Holy Spirit
27. Anointing

Chris Hogan

28. Retire Inspire
29. Everyday Millionaire

Michael Hyatt

30. Your Best Year Ever

Marina Keegan

31. The Opposite of Loneliness

Carol Ann Lee

32. Ann Frank's Story

Max Lucado

33. Grace for the Moment

C.J. Mahaney

34. Humility

John Maxwell

35. The 21 Irrefutable Laws of Leadership
36. The 21 Indispensable Qualities of a Leader

Robert Morris

37. The Blessed Marriage

Dave Ramsey

38. The Total Money Makeover
39. Complete Guide to Money
40. Baby Step Millionaire
41. The Momentum Theorem

Clay Scoggins

42. How to Lead When You're Not In Charge
43. How to Lead in a World of Distraction

Charles Stanley

44. Landmines
45. On Holy Ground
46. Pathways to His Presence
47. Surviving in the Angry World

Charles R. Swindoll

48. Joseph

Neil Clark Warren

49. Finding the Love of Your Life

Rick Warren

50. The Purpose-Driven Life

Martijn Van Tilborgh

51. Unleashed

ENDNOTES

1 Charles F. Stanley, Life Principles Bible (Nashville, TN: Thomas Nelson Inc., January 1, 2009), 1,984.

2 Stanley, Life Principles Bible, 5,019.

3 Stanley, Life Principles Bible, 1,381.

4 Sam Chand, Leadership Pain: The Classroom for Growth (Nashville, TN: Thomas Nelson, April 7, 2015), 126.

5 Dr. Henry Cloud, "Our ability to give and respond to love is our greatest gift. The heart that God has fashioned in his image is the center of our being. Its abilities to open up to love and allow love to flow outward are crucial to life. We need to claim our hearts as our property and work on our weaknesses. Doing so opens us up to life," wall post, Facebook, 29 Feb. 2020, https://www.facebook.com/photo/?fbid=10158194131079571&set=a.489655829570.

6 Donald Colbert, The Seven Pillars of Health: The Natural Way to Better Help for Life (Siloam, December 11, 2006), 243.

7 Bill Bright, Promises: A Daily Guide to Supernatural Living (New Life Publications, January 1, 2002).

8 Colbert, The Seven Pillars of Health, 235.

9 Colbert, 235.

10 Colbert, The Seven Pillars of Health, 236.

11 Colbert, 237.

12 Robert and Debbie Morris, The Blessed Marriage (Southlake, TX: Gateway Church, September 15, 2009), 177.

13 Stanley, Life Principles Bible, 4,487.

14 Stanley, Life Principles Bible, 2,184.

15 Stanley, 7,189.

16 Stanley, 825.

17 John Bevere, "There is absolutely nothing good for your life that is outside of God," wall post, Facebook, 29 Aug. 2016, https://www.facebook.com/photo/?fbid=10154501516918011&set=a.175418183010.

18 Stanley, Life Principles Bible, 244.

19 WordReference Online, s.v. "redeemed," accessed April 29, 2024, https://www.wordreference.com/definition/redeeming.

20 John Bevere, Extraordinary: The Life You're Meant to Live (Colorado Springs, CO: Waterbrook Press, 2010), 244.

21 Bevere, 118.

22 Bevere, 119.

23 Bevere, 104.

24 Bevere, Extraordinary, 120.

25 James Robinson endorsement cited in John Bevere, Extraordinary.

26 Bevere, Extraordinary, 142.

27 Stanley, Life Principles Bible, 1,470.

28 Maury Davis, The Last Ride: Finding Life's Legacy on America's Greatest Road Trip (Nashville, TN: MDM Books, 2017), 408.

29 Stanley, Life Principles Bible, 865.

30 Stanley, Life Principles Bible, 5,031.

31 Stanley, 4,644.

32 Stanley, Life Principles Bible, 1,386-1,387.

33 Stanley, Life Principles Bible, 3,954.

34 "Cedar," Woodland Trust, accessed May 1, 2024, https://www.woodlandtrust.org.uk/trees-woods-and-wildlife/british-trees/a-z-of-british-trees/cedar/.

35 Dr. Caroline Leaf, "It's Ok to Be Sad After Making the Right Decision" wall post, Facebook, 1 October 2021, https://www.facebook.com/photo/?fbid=411967186951129&set=a.265147228299793.

36 Stanley, Life Principles Bible, 28.

37 Stanley, Life Principles Bible, 3,876.

38 Stanley, 28.

39 Stanley, 241.

40 Stanley, Life Principles Bible, 4, 133.

41 Steven Furtick, "Your greatest wisdom might come after your biggest mistake. If you find yourself in failure, move forward. Better is ahead of you," wall post, Facebook, 7 December 2020, https://www.facebook.com/watch/?v=2788482161370534.

42 Bevere, Relentless, 74.

43 Bevere, Relentless, 191.

44 Stanley, Life Principles Bible, 4,677.

45 Susie Moore, Stop Checking Your Likes: Shake Off the Need for Approval and Live an Incredible Life (Novato, CA: New World Library, April 7, 2020).

46 Dr. Keith Johnson, Financial Fast Track: How to Experience Abundance, Accelerate Results, Eliminate Bad Debt (Nassau, Bahamas: Inspire, February 28, 2022).

47 Stanley, The Life Principles Bible, 758.

48 Steven Furtick, "You have an appointment in the storm," wall post, Facebook, 24 May 2020, https://www.facebook.com/StevenFurtick/videos/676131403208740/.

49 Stanley, Life Principles Bible, 1,544.

50 Steven Furtick, "It's Evident That God's Presence Has Been With Us Every Step of the Way" wall post, Facebook, 4 January 2021, https://www.facebook.com/StevenFurtick/photos/a.476017615752992/3794842770537110/?type=3.

51 Stanley, Life Principles Bible, 3,916-3,917.

52 Steffany Gretzinger and Melissa Helser, vocalists, "Give Thanks' by Henry Smith, released November 5, 2021, track 6 on Faith of My Father, Integrity's Hosanna! Music.

53 Stanley, Life Principles Bible, 831.

54 Stanley, 7.

55 Seth Godin endorsement, cited in Michael Hyatt, Your Best Year Ever: A 5-Step Plan for Achieving Your Most Important Goals (Ada, Michigan: Baker Books, November 15, 2023).

56 Stanley, Life Principles Bible. 4,228.

57 Stanley, 4,227.

58 Stanley, Life Principles Bible, 360.

59 Gary Chapman and Jocelyn Green, The 5 Love Language Military Edition: The Secret to Love That Lasts (Chicago, IL: Northfield Publishing, January 3, 2017), 180.

60 Chapman, 180.

61 Chapman, 180

62 Stanley, Life Principles Bible, 4,153.

63 Stanley, 2,133.

64 Cloud, Boundaries in Dating, 75.

65 Stanley, Life Principles Bible, 462.

66 Stanley, 6,597-6,599.

67 Stanley, Life Principles Bible, 1,387.

68 Thesaurus.com, s.v. "best," accessed May 2, 2024, https://www.thesaurus.com/browse/best.

69 Dictionary.com, s.v. "best," accessed June 4, 2024, https://www.dictionary.com/browse/best.

70 Stanley, Life Principles Bible, 6, 359.

71 Bevere, Relentless.

72 Dexter Quito, "Your joy is critical. If you maintain your joy, you win," wall post, Facebook, https://www.facebook.com/photo/?fbid=2015518615182301&set=a.1070200956380743.

73 Bevere, Relentless.

74 Johnson, Financial Fast Track, 115.

Printed in the USA
CPSIA information can be obtained
at www.ICGtesting.com
LVHW021408310824
789685LV00005B/22

9 781962 401692